AN OLD TESTA...

FEET*of* CLAY

Failures from Yesterday,
New Mercies for Today

TOBY SHOCKEY

RIVERSTONE GROUP
PUBLISHING

DEDICATION

To Crossroads Christian Fellowship,

Serving as your pastor continues to be a blessing and labor of love. We each have our own faith and relationship with God, but the living out of our faith is a "team sport." May we all run with endurance and finish the race well.

Feet of Clay – Failures from Yesterday, New Mercies for Today by Toby Shockey

Copyright © 2022. All rights reserved, including the right to reproduce this book or portions thereof in any form whatsoever. Toby Shockey

For information, contact the author at:

www.tobyshockey.com or www.mountaintime.org

ISBN: 979-8-9857349-7-3

Riverstone Group Publishing

Manufactured in the United States of America

Photo of the author by Nico Zinsmeyer

All Scripture quotations are from The Holy Bible, English Standard Version. ESV® Text Edition: 2016. Copyright © 2001 by Crossway Bibles, a publishing ministry of Good News Publishers.

CONTENTS

FOREWORD

I have said many times that a major regret, during almost 20 years as a college president, was not having had the opportunity to enter deep discussions with students - a "plus" for faculty members that keeps them in classrooms despite poor pay. But that's a whole 'nuther story.

In some cases, students "stood out," accomplishing greatly in their collegiate pilgrimage - often with trophies, citations and honors befitting their college years.

Toby Shockey was not one of those. He seemed to go about college life quietly, carving words carefully - if speaking at all - and seemingly partaking of whatever good might be extracted from what he heard or read.

It was probably during his senior year. We had exchanged greetings on many occasions and had engaged in short conversations. One day I asked, "Toby, have you made all A's in college?" I was half-kidding, knowing that few do. He paused thoughtfully, finally answering, "Yes, so far." (I've never heard a question answered so humbly, yet he smiled with the assurance that he'd have it no other way!)

He had my immense respect as a student - the kind that is ever-growing. In the years since college, it is readily apparent that I - and others whose lives he touches - would do well to heed his analytical instruction - particularly from his books, as well as verbally from pulpits. His writing is beyond brilliant. He turns phrases in ways that playwrights and other authors (including me) wish they could!

Shockey has given the Old Testament fresh air. He skillfully shows through descriptions of major Biblical figures – and particularly their failures - how much they were like us or, more accurately, how much we are like them.

Then, now and until Jesus comes, we who all fall short – as mortals are destined to do - are challenged to overcome "our ways" and seek God's way, the one which is always best. Shockey induces frowns from sharp focus on many Old Testament figures, but grins aren't far behind. His messages point to the hope, promises and assurances by the Maker and Master of all. I hope he will always be challenged to write. I will always readily read his work, applying it as I can even in twilight years.

–Dr. Don Newbury
Chancellor, Howard Payne University

INTRODUCTION

Y ou've probably seen some of the memes making the rounds in social media with the caption, "You Had One Job" along with the photographic evidence of someone's inability to complete a simple task. Maybe the person who painted "SOTP" at the crosswalk was simply having an off day. Perhaps the poor soul who labeled the corn on the cob as "watermelon" didn't have their glasses or their coffee. Failure can be hilarious – at least when someone else is doing the failing.

The Old Testament is a continuous story of failure, but the failure wasn't nearly as amusing. Even with the Psalms that comfort us, the Proverbs that enlighten us and all of the stories that inspire us, "You Had One Job" would still be a viable caption for that first part of our Bibles.

Jesus was once asked about the greatest commandment in all of Scripture. If He had to boil it all down, what did God want from His people? Matthew 22:37–38 tells us, "And he said to him, 'You shall love the Lord your God with all your heart and with all your soul and with all your mind. This is the great and first commandment.'" But Jesus wasn't issuing a new commandment; He was simply quoting the Old Testament. Deuteronomy 6:4–5 says, "Hear, O Israel: The LORD our God, the LORD is one. You shall love the LORD your God with all your heart and with all your soul and with all your might."

But, in large measure, they didn't. A few heroes - like Joseph and Daniel - demonstrated their love for God even as they endured dark and difficult days, but so many others had golden opportunities to trust and honor the Lord and failed miserably. Even the most essential, pivotal characters in the Old Testament - men such as Abraham, Moses and David on occasion - found a way to snatch defeat out of the jaws of victory.

Thankfully, God had a plan all along. The whole trajectory of the Old Testament points to and prepares the way for Jesus. In fact, we miss the point if we don't read the Old Testament in the light of Jesus and through the lens of the New Testament. The ongoing saga of repeated and predictable failure served to prepare the way for Jesus. People would not and could not keep God's laws, so God sent Jesus to do what they (and we) could never do.

But despite the epic failures and the ugly truths ever so present in the lives of the people of Israel, the Holy Spirit inspired the Scriptures – including the **Old** Testament – for us to read and ponder and learn to love God even more. No, they didn't get it right; but neither have we. Back then, the righteous looked forward to the coming of the Savior; but today we strive to live in the victory of "It is finished" (John 19:30). As we fight not for victory but *from* victory, may the examples from the lives of the people in the Old Testament give us wisdom and warning. Although they lived thousands of years before us, we resemble them more than we realize.

A powerful king once had a dream that disturbed him; but when he awakened, the king could no longer remember the dream - let alone understand its meaning. But Daniel stepped forward to both reveal and interpret the dream for the king. Nebuchadnezzar had dreamed of an image - essentially a statue - but one with a frightening appearance. "The head of this image was of fine gold, its chest and arms of silver, its middle and thighs of bronze, its legs of iron, its feet partly of iron and partly of clay" (Daniel 2:32-33). Through the years, much ink has been spilled in speculation of what the various parts of the image represented, but the parts aren't as important as the rock that brought them all down. The rock crushed the feet of the image and shattered the image into pieces small enough to be blown away in the wind. The rock was victorious over the statue, likely signifying that the Kingdom of God will topple all the kingdoms of this world – past, present and future.

When we see a person of great strength and ability but also with a fatal flaw, it's often said that they have "feet of clay." Did you know that expression came from the Bible? We have certainly seen people with feet of clay - much like the statue. The heroes of the Bible also had great strengths and abilities and were used by the Lord to do wonderful things, but their stories are not preserved for us without including their struggles and failures. The statue wasn't the only one with feet of clay.

The unsettling aspect of all this is that - in the stories of these characters - we find striking parallels to our own lives. Careful study of their lives reveals similarities that hit way too close to home. Even as we are continually being changed into the image of Christ, all too often and in so many ways, we too have feet of clay.

So why study failure? Why focus on what went wrong? Because we have much to glean from their mistakes in hopes of not repeating them. More importantly, we're reminded again and again that failure was superseded by grace. All their inabilities - and an honest consideration of our own - point us to Jesus, the One who was pierced for our transgressions and crushed for our iniquities. Even in the darkness, the Light shines. Where we all failed, Jesus conquered. Romans 15:4 reminds us, "For whatever was written in former days was written for our instruction, that through endurance and through the encouragement of the Scriptures we might have hope." May the Lord fill you with His hope as you study His Word.

–Toby Shockey
www.mountaintime.org
www.tobyshockey.com

NOAH: BESETTING SIN, RESETTING SIN

READING: GENESIS 9

FOCUS: *Genesis 9:20–21 "Noah began to be a man of the soil, and he planted a vineyard. He drank of the wine and became drunk and lay uncovered in his tent."*

As we witness the decline and deterioration of our society, maybe you've wondered how modern times compare to the days of Noah leading up to the great flood. Today even the covenant sign of the rainbow has been hijacked for ungodly purposes. Noah was and is one of the heroes of the faith. Hebrews 11:7 sums up his story, "By faith Noah, being warned by God concerning events as yet unseen, in reverent fear constructed an ark for the saving of his household. By this he condemned the world and became an heir of the righteousness that comes by faith." Peter referred to Noah as a "herald of righteousness" (2 Peter 2:5). The Bible also tells us that "Noah was a righteous man, blameless in his generation. Noah walked with God" (Genesis 6:9).

For all those reasons, what Noah did after the rainbow is truly strange and surprising. Before we get to that, let's first note that this story did not have to be included in Scripture at all. Thousands of years later, Noah remains more known for what he did before and during the flood than for what he did after. But the Bible doesn't hide the flaws, the weaknesses and the massive failures of the faithful. Overall, Noah's life was stellar - a prime example of trust and obedience. But on one occasion, Noah blew it badly. The bottom line, without an especially nice way to say this, is that Noah got drunk and made a fool of himself. In the process, Noah also embarrassed his family. "Noah began to be a

13

man of the soil, and he planted a vineyard. He drank of the wine and became drunk and lay uncovered in his tent" (Genesis 9:20–21). The tense of the verb reveals that Noah wasn't just uncovered but that he had uncovered himself. You probably don't remember singing about that part of the story in *Arky, Arky.*

Noah wouldn't be the last person ever to make regrettable decisions because he had too much to drink, but his actions proved to be more revealing than the clothes he wasn't wearing. Remember that God had just finished destroying the world with a flood because of sin. This was a fresh start, a new day. Adam and Eve had previously ruined the world, but now there was another chance. But the mud probably hadn't even dried yet before Noah demonstrated that the sin and foolishness in the human heart had survived the flood along with all the animals.

But Noah was not the only one who was exposed by the entire situation. "And Ham, the father of Canaan, saw the nakedness of his father and told his two brothers outside" (Genesis 9:22). The speculation about what "saw the nakedness" means and what Ham actually did to Noah here runs the gamut from sodomy to incest with his mother. But those conclusions are unlikely and unnecessary. What is certain is that Ham dishonored his father. Ham was responsible for his own actions, but this wouldn't have happened without Noah's drunkenness. Ham didn't grieve the foolishness of Noah but reveled in the opportunity to mock his father and broadcast Noah's shameful condition. In contrast, we see that this was no cause for celebration for Noah's other sons. "Then Shem and Japheth took a garment, laid it on both their shoulders, and walked backward and covered the nakedness of their father. Their faces were turned backward, and they did not see their father's nakedness" (Genesis 9:23). To describe the situation as "awkward" would be an understatement.

Shem and Japheth honored the dishonored Noah by attempting to cover his disgrace rather than draw attention to it. We are left to wonder about some of the details; but after Noah sobered up, he knew which sons had honored him and which son had disgraced him. Noah spoke blessings over Shem and Japheth; but in another plot twist, Noah did not curse Ham but rather Canaan, one of Ham's sons. "Cursed be Canaan; a servant of servants shall he be to his brothers" (Genesis 9:25). Many years later, the Israelites would seek to drive the Canaanites out from the land God was giving to them; but the Canaanites and their false gods would never cease to be thorns in their sides.

Whether or not you consume alcohol isn't really the issue here. As with many other decisions, know your Bible, follow the leading of the Spirit and don't violate your own conscience. Obviously, nothing good happens from drunkenness; and Noah would live out his days embarrassed over his choices. But more than a temperance lecture, Noah's story is a warning to us about our own vulnerability. Even the one the Bible calls "the herald of righteousness" was vulnerable. Noah was around 600 years old after the flood and nearing the third trimester of his life. He knew better, but he didn't do better. We would like to think that we can finally mature beyond the point of being vulnerable to temptation in certain areas; but if Noah could fail so ingloriously, what makes us think that we couldn't? Walk wisely. Walk humbly.

"Keep your heart with all vigilance, for from it flow the springs of life."
Proverbs 4:23

HEAD TO HEART

- To what areas of sin are you especially vulnerable? And not vulnerable?

- What attitudes or conditions make us more susceptible to temptations?

- Have you been tempted to secretly rejoice when someone else fails badly?

THE "BABEL-ERS": DELUSION AND CONFUSION

READING: GENESIS 11

FOCUS: *Genesis 11:9 "Therefore its name was called Babel, because there the LORD confused the language of all the earth. And from there the LORD dispersed them over the face of all the earth."*

We don't hear much about the story of the Tower of Babel, and that could be because the events that unfolded are rather strange. Isn't the whole idea of building a tower with its top in the heavens pretty ridiculous? Shouldn't they have realized that reaching the heavens was never going to happen? Yes, their idea was ridiculous; but not for the reasons we might assume. We might think of them as being primitive, but most people today live by the same goals and ambitions.

When God first created the man and the woman and again after the flood, God commanded people to be fruitful and multiply and fill the earth. The generations that followed Noah were doing this until some decided they did not want to be dispersed. That desire can seem noble - like a warm and fuzzy desire for togetherness, but living in harmony wasn't the real motivation. At the heart of their desire to come together was the ambition to make a name for themselves. "Then they said, 'Come, let us build ourselves a city and a tower with its top in the heavens, and let us make a name for ourselves, lest we be dispersed over the face of the whole earth'" (Genesis 11:4). By seeking to make a name for themselves and in building themselves a city, the people on the plain in Shinar were really attempting to establish a civilization without God.

In defiance of God's command to fill the earth, they wanted to centralize, build and achieve on their own - independent of God and His design for the world He created. This was one of the earliest attempts of man to make himself a god rather than submit to his Creator. When we understand that the building of the city and tower represented independence from God, we also see that - in different ways - people are trying to achieve the same ends today. As much as we might enjoy the conveniences that technology affords us, hasn't it also influenced the prevalent notion that man can accomplish anything? People today believe the same lie that they were believing back then: we don't need God because we are all we need.

Debate surrounds what the people of Shinar actually built, and we are not given the specifics of what they did or did not accomplish. The rest of the story shows that none of their efforts were expended to glorify God. They wanted to make a name for themselves. They wanted to show that together they could accomplish anything. They wanted to be God.

Was God concerned that they could reach the heavens? Was God at all threatened by what they could achieve together? Notice the wording of this verse. "And the LORD came down to see the city and the tower, which the children of man had built" (Genesis 11:5). Now we understand that the Bible is using figurative language here. God didn't have to actually "come down" to see their building since He is omniscient; but the idea is that - whatever they built - God still had to come down to their level. Despite their best efforts and all their togetherness, whatever they built or achieved fell pathetically short of God.

The whole thing would be comical except that God knew what man could and would accomplish without Him - evil followed by even greater evil. God was never in danger of being unseated as God, but He knew the depths of man's depravity and would not allow this to continue. "And the LORD said, 'Behold, they are one people, and they have all one language, and this is only the beginning of what they will do. And nothing that they propose to do will now be impossible for them'" (Genesis 11:6). What the people saw as "progress" had to stop. "'Come, let us go down and there confuse their language, so that they may not understand one another's speech.' So the LORD dispersed them from there over the face of all the earth, and they left off building the city. Therefore its name was called Babel, because there the LORD confused the language of all the earth. And from there the LORD dispersed them over the face of all the earth" (Genesis 11:7–9).

Ever since that time, man has been attempting the same scheme in different ways. History has been one reenactment of the Tower of Babel after another. People try to live without God, and God allows them to go so far before He intervenes. World empires rise and fall. Rulers come and go. We see cycles and patterns in human history because of the clash between man's determination to live apart from God and God's insistence that this is still His world. Man will never be God; but through Jesus, we can know God. We can never reach Heaven by our own ingenuity or accomplishments, but we can become citizens of heaven by grace through faith. We don't need to build a city because God has built one for us. There is one God, and we aren't Him.

"Why do the nations rage and the peoples plot in vain? . . .
He who sits in the heavens laughs; the Lord holds them in derision."
Psalm 2:1, 4

HEAD TO HEART

- In what ways do you see people trying to live as though God doesn't exist today?

- What drives people to want to live without God? Is that their own choice or God's?

- In what ways have you tried to live independent of God and perhaps learned the hard way?

ABRAM: THE PRICE OF PANIC

READING: GENESIS 12:10-20

FOCUS: *Genesis 12:13 "Say you are my sister, that it may go well with me because of you, and that my life may be spared for your sake."*

Abram had obeyed the Lord and had set out on the journey to which God had called him; but when famine afflicted the land, we can understand his dilemma. With his family to feed, Abram understandably must've thought to himself, "I've got to do something. I can't let everyone starve." The problem emerged when Abram decided to "just do something" instead of trusting in the Lord.

Because the famine was so severe, Abram's solution was to take his family down to Egypt. Now this was long before Moses, Pharaoh and all the plagues; so Egypt wasn't necessarily a terrible place, and at least they had food there. But there was no indication that God led or wanted Abram to go to Egypt. From all appearances, Abram panicked and ran away. The policy of "it's easier to get forgiveness than permission" should never apply to our relationship with God. As you have no doubt discovered, sometimes we create more problems when we take the wrong approach to solving the original problem. Yes, there might've been more food in Egypt; but their arrival in Egypt only produced a new set of problems.

When Abram told his wife Sarai, "I know that you are a woman beautiful in appearance," he wasn't being romantic but practical. Because Sarai was attractive, Abram realized that he could be killed and Sarai forced into marrying an Egyptian. Suddenly the famine didn't seem like such a huge problem. Truly Abram had traded one set of problems for another, which is what usually happens when we trust our own vast wisdom instead of seeking the Lord.

If we're keeping score here, Abram's life was potentially threatened by the famine; so he went to Egypt where his life was definitely threatened by the Egyptians. So Abram told Sarai to lie, but it wasn't a complete lie. (Isn't it interesting that we refer to this as a "half-truth" instead of a "half-lie"?) "Say you are my sister, that it may go well with me because of you, and that my life may be spared for your sake" (Genesis 12:13).

Strangely enough, Sarai was indeed Abram's half-sister, who also happened to be his wife. (Genesis 20:12) Today we're repulsed by the idea of inbreeding, but marriage within the family was the norm in those days. Abram's fears were realized when the Egyptian pharaoh took Sarai into his home with apparent intentions for her. When the full truth emerged, Abram had to confess his dishonesty and was told to get out of Egypt.

The entire situation was avoidable; and although Abram acquired wealth in Egypt, he had put his family at risk through his foolish scheme to save them. What do we learn from Abram's example? *When you go where you aren't supposed to go, you'll do what you aren't supposed to do.* This principle proves true in a variety of situations - whether we're considering a major life move or simply a questionable activity. The first domino falls when we put ourselves in a place where we shouldn't be.

However, this was not the only time that Abram (later Abraham) pulled the same stunt. In Genesis 20, Abraham used the same "she's my sister" strategy with another king with predictably similar results. Abraham evidently didn't learn anything the first time. But before we're too critical, have you ever repeated the same mistake or tried the same strategy that already failed before?

Later, we read that Sarai had a maidservant named Hagar. The Bible also mentions that Hagar was an Egyptian, so it's entirely possible that

Hagar entered the lives of Abram and Sarai during this time in Egypt. The day would come when both would regret involving Hagar in their lives. (Genesis 16) Sometimes the consequences continue long after the choices are made and regretted.

Before you panic, before you "just do something," do everything you can to ensure you're following God's leading. If you don't have that assurance, wait until you do. The consequences from which you can save yourself are well worth the wait.

> *"Trust in the LORD with all your heart,*
> *and do not lean on your own understanding."*
> Proverbs 3:5

HEAD TO HEART

- Have you made any costly decisions because you panicked and reacted poorly?

- In what ways have you been tempted to withhold information or tell half-truths to make things easier for yourself?

- Why does putting yourself in a bad situation increase the likelihood that you'll make more bad decisions?

SARAI: HELPING GOD KEEP HIS WORD

READING: GENESIS 16

FOCUS: *Genesis 16:2 "And Sarai said to Abram, 'Behold now, the LORD has prevented me from bearing children. Go in to my servant; it may be that I shall obtain children by her.' And Abram listened to the voice of Sarai."*

You may have already noticed that there are not many women in our study, which speaks rather favorably of the women in the Old Testament. Given the frequency and the extent of the failures of the men, the women barely qualify. But even as we consider Sarai, we need to remember that she had significant help from her husband Abram in making her colossal blunder. Sarai, however, can be rightfully credited with having one of the worst ideas in the entire history of really bad ideas.

Perhaps the condition is worse today than ever before, but humans have never excelled at waiting. We want what we want, and we want it now but preferably sooner. One of the luxuries that God has in being the Eternal One is that He never has to be in a rush; time is never a limiting factor for God. If it seems to us like God is not in a hurry, be assured that He isn't.

When God promised Abram that his descendants would be as numerous as the stars in the sky, Abram believed Him. What Abram could not have understood is how long the wait would be between promise and fulfillment. In all fairness to Abram and Sarai, they were more patient than any of us would likely have been. But as many as 10 years had passed since God's promise (Genesis 12:4-5, 16:16); and neither Abram nor Sarai was getting any younger. They may not have understood all the implications of God's promise; but they did understand that to eventually have numerous descendants, they had to start with one. But year after year, they remained childless.

Maybe the idea came to her gradually or maybe instantly, but Sarai had a notion. Surely, they'd given God enough time; so the time had come to help Him out. "Now Sarai, Abram's wife, had borne him no children. She had a female Egyptian servant whose name was Hagar. And Sarai said to Abram, 'Behold now, the LORD has prevented me from bearing children. Go in to my servant; it may be that I shall obtain children by her.' And Abram listened to the voice of Sarai" (Genesis 16:1–2).

Undoubtedly, Sarai was in a dire situation and increasingly so as the years passed; but this was not the solution. If there had ever been a time for Abram not to be a dutiful husband, this would have been that time. But whether Abram was reluctant or all too eager, he complied.

We can always see things more clearly in hindsight, but a gift of prophecy wasn't necessary to see that this was all going to go badly. In fact, Ishmael had not even been born yet when things began to fall apart. "And he went in to Hagar, and she conceived. And when she saw that she had conceived, she looked with contempt on her mistress" (Genesis 16:4). While this was sad for Sarai, what did she think was going to happen? How would there not be drama, resentment and all kinds of awkwardness in this whole ill-conceived arrangement? Not surprisingly, Sarai then treated Hagar harshly to the point that she had to take the child and flee.

The story unfolds over time and in greater detail, but even that portion of the whole gives us plenty to ponder. If you know the rest of the story, God still kept His promise to Abram and Sarai. Their impatience did not negate God's faithfulness. God didn't walk away from His commitment because they foolishly tried to go around Him. Isaac was born to Abraham and Sarah in their old age as the child of God's promise and the source of joyful laughter.

Are you in a season of waiting on God? Are there promises not yet fulfilled? Waiting is beyond difficult because the delay often exposes some unpleasant realities. Maybe we trust in God's blessings more than we trust His heart. Maybe we've made an idol out of our desire, believing that if only we had *that*, then we could be content. But is God enough? Our impatience reveals that we really do believe that we know better than God.

But as you wait and hold fast to His Word, learn from Sarai. You will never need to violate God's commands to achieve God's purposes. You won't get there faster by trying to go around God. While our obedience may be required, He is never in need of our assistance. Impatience and our manipulative attempts to speed things along only create heartache. Resting in the assurance that God always keeps His promises, may we have the grace to wait well.

> *"I wait for the LORD, my soul waits, and in his word I hope."*
> Psalm 130:5

HEAD TO HEART

- What promises of God have you seen come to fulfillment in your life?

- What promises are you still waiting to see fulfilled?

- What has been the biggest temptation to try to "help God" make things happen?

ISAAC: SISTER ACT TOO

READING: GENESIS 26

FOCUS: *Genesis 26:7 "When the men of the place asked him about his wife, he said, 'She is my sister,' for he feared to say, 'My wife,' thinking, 'lest the men of the place should kill me because of Rebekah,' because she was attractive in appearance."*

If you had a friend who made a big mistake, would you try the same thing just to see if you got the same consequences? If your friend then made the same mistake again with the same bad outcome, would you still do the same thing and hope for a better result? The answers seem so obvious and simple, but life experience proves otherwise. Because we are so flawed and sinful, we tend to repeat not only our own mistakes but also the avoidable mistakes of others.

From the category of "you can't even make this up," Isaac, the son of Abram and Sarai (later called Abraham and Sarah), told the same lie about his wife being his sister that Abram had twice told about Sarai. And Isaac told the same lie for the same reason: his wife Rebekah was attractive, so Isaac feared for his life. To add to the irony, Abraham had already told the same "half-truth" to the same king, Abimelech of Gerar (or at least a son or grandson of his with the same name).

We can congratulate Abraham and Isaac for their good eyesight in the selection of their wives, but they both needed a better strategy for protecting themselves and their trophy wives in a foreign land. Isaac's situation was different from his father's because he could at least say that he was where he was supposed to be. Even though Isaac was on his way to Egypt, God told him to stay in Gerar, and he did. With the instructions to remain in Gerar, God also reminded and reaffirmed

29

for Isaac the covenant promises that He had made to Abraham. "I will multiply your offspring as the stars of heaven and will give to your offspring all these lands. And in your offspring all the nations of the earth shall be blessed" (Genesis 26:4). The promises were for Isaac, too.

So Isaac knew he was where God wanted him to be, and he knew that God had promised to multiply his offspring. We can also assume that Isaac realized his survival and Rebekah's survival were necessary for the fulfillment of God's promises. Considering these factors, wasn't God going to protect them? Would God fail to preserve them and thus break His covenant?

After implementing the same "she's my sister" ploy, Isaac's lie was revealed. The strategy hadn't worked before; why would it be effective this time? Genesis 26:8 says, "When he had been there a long time, Abimelech king of the Philistines looked out of a window and saw Isaac laughing with Rebekah his wife." Understand the Hebrew word for "laughing" suggests more intimacy than a few shared chuckles. Whatever Abimelech observed, he knew immediately that Isaac and Rebekah weren't siblings. Maybe they came from a close family but not *that* close.

Abimelech was horrified at the prospect of what could have happened due to Isaac's dishonesty and pledged to protect both Isaac and Rebekah in his land. Ironically, the foreign king was the one who acted with integrity. The story ends on a somewhat happy note, but the unnecessary drama could have been avoided if Isaac had simply trusted God in the first place.

We shake our heads at the foolishness of the lies that were told and the sins that were repeated. We're even tempted to see ourselves as wiser and morally superior to Abraham and Isaac and all their offspring. But while they were in uncharted territory, we are not. We have what they did not have – their example from which to learn, along with a Bible full of more examples.

We tend to panic instead of trusting God; we lie instead of speaking the truth; and we trust in our own wisdom even after that wisdom has failed us many times before. History still repeats itself as we repeat the sins of our fathers - individually and corporately. Abraham, Isaac and all the rest needed a Savior. And so do we.

> *"Be not wise in your own eyes; fear the LORD,*
> *and turn away from evil."*
> Proverbs 3:7

HEAD TO HEART

- Are you aware of any sins that tend to run in your family?

- In what ways have you devised your own strategy for a situation instead of trusting God?

- When we stop believing God's promises, in what are we believing instead?

JUDAH: ALL IN THE FAMILY

READING: GENESIS 38

FOCUS: *Genesis 38:24 "About three months later Judah was told, 'Tamar your daughter-in-law has been immoral. Moreover, she is pregnant by immorality.' And Judah said, 'Bring her out, and let her be burned.'"*

More than likely, the sordid details of Genesis 38 never made it into your Sunday School curriculum; and their placement within the story of Joseph seems like an embarrassing interruption. (Genesis 37, 39-50) But isn't it like God to work through even the most awkward situations, with His plan and purpose still completely intact?

On the heels of selling Joseph into Egyptian slavery, Judah left his brothers and went and found himself a wife from among the Canaanites. Judah had apparently learned nothing from the bad example of Uncle Esau about marrying foreign women. (Genesis 26:34-35) Years passed; and to no one's surprise, Judah's sons grew up to be reprobates - so much so that God ended them. "But Er, Judah's firstborn, was wicked in the sight of the LORD, and the LORD put him to death" (Genesis 38:7). In other words, Er erred and was then "Er-adicated."

With Er out of the picture, his brother Onan was supposed to marry Er's widow Tamar and produce offspring for his late brother. In the interest of keeping this devotional "rated G," let's just say that Onan did not honor his obligation. (Genesis 38:9-10) Judah then promised his third son Shelah to Tamar but reneged on his promise, ignoring his family obligation and leaving Tamar in an impossible situation.

But Tamar was shrewd and must have known her father-in-law quite well. Judah wasn't known for making the best of choices, but no one could have anticipated the depth of the hole he was about to dig. Tamar disguised herself in such a way that Judah not only did not recognize her but also believed her to be a prostitute. Judah then secured her services with the pledge of a few possessions that could be easily identified as his until he paid her for her services. Of course, Judah didn't know she was his daughter-in-law; but he apparently wasn't considering that possibility when he was seeking to indulge himself.

Soon afterwards, Tamar realized that she was pregnant – and by her father-in-law. Not only did that reality create a terribly awkward situation for Judah, this also explains why this chapter of the Bible may not have been included in your Sunday School curriculum. When Judah tried to quietly settle his account with the prostitute and retrieve his possessions, no prostitute was to be found. Judah then sought to quietly move on and hoped to avoid a potentially embarrassing situation, but he had no idea what was coming.

Not until three months later did Judah find out that Tamar was pregnant. Without realizing the child was his, Judah's response was less than compassionate: "Bring her out and let her be burned." But Judah was the one who was about to get "burned." When Tamar produced Judah's possessions, Judah had one of the most uncomfortable moments anyone has ever endured. He was left with nothing else to say but, "She is more righteous than I, since I did not give her to my son Shelah" (Genesis 38:26). He was right that time.

About six months later, after Tamar gave birth to twin sons, the storyline abruptly shifted back to Joseph's new life in Egypt. We are left to ask what that was all about and why these sordid details were included on the pages of Scripture. No doubt Judah especially would've preferred to have kept the whole embarrassing ordeal a secret.

Obviously, Judah's story is a prime example of why sexual sin is a bad idea. No one has learned the truth that "your sins will find you out" more powerfully than Judah. Judah is also the textbook example of why Jesus would later tell some other hypocrites, "Let him who is without sin among you be the first to throw a stone at her" (John 8:7). We do well to heed Judah's bad example, but the irony and surprises aren't over.

Jacob's twelve sons, including Judah, were the fathers of the 12 tribes of Israel. When Jesus came, He was not born into the tribe of Levi, the priestly tribe. Instead Jesus was born into the tribe of *Judah*. The illegitimate twin sons of Judah and Tamar were Jesus' ancestors. More than that, Tamar the prostitute is mentioned by name in Matthew's genealogy of Jesus. (Matthew 1:3) (And you thought your family had some baggage!) Not only did Jesus come to save sinners, but He also identified Himself with them. Despite our failures and horrible choices, He is not ashamed to call us brothers and sisters. (Hebrews 2:11) Our past may not be pretty, and our present may still fall pathetically short; but Jesus became one of us to save us. Jesus, the Lion of the tribe of Judah, is redeeming your story, too.

> *"He does not deal with us according to our sins,*
> *nor repay us according to our iniquities."*
> Psalm 103:10

HEAD TO HEART

- What parts of your story are a source of embarrassment or humiliation?

- Why would God even allow things like these to happen at all? Why not intervene sooner?

- How have you seen God's mercy even in the consequences of your own sin?

MOSES: TOO MUCH, TOO SOON

READING: EXODUS 2:11-15

FOCUS: *Exodus 2:12 "He looked this way and that, and seeing no one, he struck down the Egyptian and hid him in the sand."*

The day would come when Moses would be memorialized like no other for how God used him to bring His people out of slavery. "And there has not arisen a prophet since in Israel like Moses, whom the LORD knew face to face, none like him for all the signs and the wonders that the LORD sent him to do in the land of Egypt, to Pharaoh and to all his servants and to all his land, and for all the mighty power and all the great deeds of terror that Moses did in the sight of all Israel" (Deuteronomy 34:10–12).

But that day would come later. Exodus 2 tells the well-known story of how baby Moses in the basket was rescued from the river and brought into the household of Pharaoh. The story then skips ahead 40 years. We don't know what it was like for Moses to grow up in the household of Pharaoh, but what we do see right away is that Moses still identified himself with the Hebrew people. Perhaps Moses understood the unique position that he had in effectively being both Hebrew and Egyptian. We can only wonder if Moses had already sensed a call from the Lord on behalf of His people. Whatever God had said or not said to Moses by that point, Moses had apparently had enough of the way His people were being treated by the Egyptians.

"One day, when Moses had grown up, he went out to his people and looked on their burdens, and he saw an Egyptian beating a Hebrew, one of his people. He looked this way and that, and seeing no one, he struck down the Egyptian and hid him in the sand" (Exodus 2:11–12). No one can fault Moses for being sympathetic to his kinsman and angry with the Egyptian. The New Testament retelling of these events recognizes the dilemma Moses faced. "When he was forty years old, it came into his heart to visit his brothers, the children of Israel. And seeing one of them being wronged, he defended the oppressed man and avenged him by striking down the Egyptian" (Acts 7:23–24). Truly if Moses could have received a fair trial, he might have been acquitted for a crime of passion rather than a premeditated slaying.

But even if his heart was in the right place in taking up the cause of his fellow Hebrew, Moses was wrong to take matters into his own hands. He "looked this way and that" before he killed the Egyptian and afterwards tried to hide the body because he knew this was murder. When Moses discovered that his deed had not gone unnoticed, we learn that not even his fellow Hebrew supported Moses' actions. "Who made you a prince and a judge over us? Do you mean to kill me as you killed the Egyptian?" (Exodus 2:14) When Moses knew that Pharaoh sought retaliation, he fled to Midian and remained there in the wilderness for the next 40 years of his life.

For decades, Moses was left to wonder what might have been. Was all the time he spent in Egypt now wasted? Why would God have orchestrated the events of his early life in the way that He did only to leave Moses out in the wilderness - alienated from both the Egyptians and his own people? Of course, we know that wasn't the end of the story; but even before Moses ever wandered upon the burning bush, the story of his life – up until then – is profoundly instructive.

Moses may have been ready to rescue his people, but God wasn't. God's plan all along was to rescue His people from Egypt with a strong and mighty hand, and that hand would be His own. Yes, the day would come when God would call Moses to bring His people out of Egypt; but by that time, Moses was not the same man. No longer ready to take matters into his own hands, Moses had been refined and humbled in the decades of isolation and waiting. Moses unknowingly spent two-thirds of his life preparing for a big finish. As you may have noticed in your own life, God doesn't do things the way we would do them.

This is not to suggest that God only uses old people, but many of us can remember being a lot like Moses. We had zeal and enthusiasm but lacked wisdom. Ready to charge the gates of hell with a squirt gun, we couldn't understand why God didn't seem to be cooperating with our plans to build His Kingdom . . . and perhaps our own kingdom, too. But God was protecting us (and surely many others!). We thought we were ready when God knew that we weren't. Our wilderness may be in a different location, but the wilderness experience still happens for those whom God is preparing.

Maybe you're there now. You want to do great things for God. You want to see Him use you in powerful ways. But today is the "day of small things." Moses could have never dreamed what God was preparing *for* him, but God had to prepare Moses first. The process is long, arduous and many times tedious; but never cease to be amazed that God can and will use someone like you – in His time and in His way.

> *"Now the man Moses was very meek,*
> *more than all people who were on the face of the earth."*
> Numbers 12:3

HEAD TO HEART

- What season of your life would you call your wilderness experience? Are you there now?

- Why would God wait 40 more years to rescue His people if life was difficult for them already?

- In what ways has God protected you from yourself when you lacked wisdom?

NADAB & ABIHU: WORSHIP IN YOUR OWN WAY

READING: LEVITICUS 10

FOCUS: *Leviticus 10:2 "And fire came out from before the LORD and consumed them, and they died before the LORD."*

Imagine a routine Sunday morning worship service. The usual crowd. A couple of up-tempo praise songs followed by some slower choruses with the occasional traditional hymn. Many are singing along but few with any fervor. Nearly everyone is preoccupied with distracting thoughts. *I'm so over this song. . . . Why would she wear that again? . . . I hope he doesn't preach so long this week. . . . What time's the game? . . . This next week is going to be the worst.* The approach to worship is casual – if not flippant; but God is just happy we're all here, right? We could have done something else, but here we are attending a worship service. Good for us. Suddenly a ball of fire comes through the ceiling and instantly incinerates the entire middle section. People die. The service comes to a halt; and out of sheer terror, no one can speak. And none of this was even in the bulletin.

The scenario seems far-fetched and hard to envision, but is our approach to the worship of Almighty God casual and flippant? Is our intensity (or lack of intensity) based more on our convenience and worship style preferences than the character and attributes of God? God's patience and mercy are demonstrated on a weekly basis in that He doesn't bring a sudden, wrathful end to so much of what is called worship.

On our best day, what we have to offer to God falls pathetically short of what He deserves; but that doesn't justify our apathy. From the glimpses of heaven that we see in Scripture, worship is both glorious and continuous. But even in this world, worship is essential. We worship Him because He is worthy. We worship Him because we experience His presence and His goodness as we set our minds and hearts on Him in worship. In fact, we were created to worship, and we will inevitably worship someone or something. All idolatry - whether it's bowing to a golden calf in the Old Testament or living for the approval of others today - is simply misdirected worship.

The worship practices in the Old Testament are foreign to us. We are eternally thankful that Jesus' ultimate sacrifice eliminated the need for the sacrificial system. We are also thankful that the Holy Spirit has now come to dwell in the hearts of His children instead of a tent or a church building. But if there is one thing that we need to grasp from the Old Testament concerning worship, we must see that God is still to be feared and deeply reverenced. He has displayed His great love for us in Jesus, but He is awesome and holy. Since God never changes and cannot change, He is the same God in both the Old and New Testaments.

One fateful day in the years between the Exodus and entering the Promised Land, the sons of Aaron failed to honor God's holiness. They decided to make an offering in the way they saw fit rather than in the way that God had prescribed. "Now Nadab and Abihu, the sons of Aaron, each took his censer and put fire in it and laid incense on it and offered unauthorized fire before the LORD, which he had not commanded them" (Leviticus 10:1). Some of the older translations refer to this as "strange fire."

The task was to take coals from the altar and place them in an incense container called a censer. The burning of incense represented the rising of the prayers and worship of God's people. We are not certain as to exactly what Nadab and Abihu did that made the fire strange, but we can safely assume that they simply decided to do things their own way instead of what was commanded. What is certain is that the strange fire was met with a consuming fire. "And fire came out from before the LORD and consumed them, and they died before the LORD" (Leviticus 10:2). The details of the offering may have seemed pointless or trivial to Nadab and Abihu and possibly to us as well, but they were important to God.

From the response of Moses and Aaron, we get a little more context for what happened and why. "Then Moses said to Aaron, 'This is what the LORD has said: "Among those who are near me I will be sanctified, and before all the people I will be glorified."' And Aaron held his peace" (Leviticus 10:3). Nadab and Abihu had an important role in the service of the Lord, but they apparently failed to see the seriousness of what they had been commanded to do.

We can and should be joyful in worship, but celebration and deep reverence are not mutually exclusive. Through Jesus, we come to God in awe and reverence - not because we fear He might incinerate us but because He is worthy. May God grant us repentance for the times when our worship has been self-centered and half-hearted. May our worship be fitting for the glorious God we adore.

"And one called to another and said: 'Holy, holy, holy is the LORD of hosts; the whole earth is full of his glory!' And the foundations of the thresholds shook at the voice of him who called, and the house was filled with smoke. And I said: 'Woe is me! For I am lost; for I am a man of unclean lips, and I dwell in the midst of a people of unclean lips; for my eyes have seen the King, the LORD of hosts!'"
Isaiah 6:3-5

HEAD TO HEART

- What are some of the things that help you sense God's presence in times of worship?

- What can you do when you don't "feel" like worshipping?

- What are some of the attributes/characteristics of God that you tend to forget or neglect?

KORAH: THE HUMBLING
OF GRUMBLING

READING: NUMBERS 16

FOCUS: *Numbers 16:30 "But if the LORD creates something new, and the ground opens its mouth and swallows them up with all that belongs to them, and they go down alive into Sheol, then you shall know that these men have despised the LORD."*

If anyone has ever experienced the heavy burden of leadership, Moses surely did. Perhaps better than anyone else, Moses knew that leading people - even God's people - is not for the faint of heart. But as a leader, Moses had one essential thing going for him. Moses had been appointed by God to lead His people during those pivotal years. His authority was not self-derived but entrusted to him by God. Many times, Moses likely would have been happy to hand over the keys to someone else.

Knowing what we know about Moses, we might wonder who in their right mind would have the audacity to question Moses' leadership. Didn't they know about "I AM" appearing to Moses in the burning bush? Didn't they remember all the plagues on Egypt and crossing the Red Sea on dry land? But as you have probably noticed, people are funny and not always in amusing ways. Korah decided that Moses was out of line and that Aaron was not fit to serve as the high priest. Worse than that, Korah influenced many others to reach the same conclusions. "They assembled themselves together against Moses and against Aaron and said to them, 'You have gone too far! For all in the congregation are holy, every one of them, and the LORD is among them. Why then do you exalt yourselves above the assembly of the LORD?'" (Numbers 16:3)

Like the cults and other fringe movements, Korah and the others began with a truthful premise but then jumped to a false conclusion. Yes, God was among all His people; and they were all a "kingdom of priests" (Exodus 19:6); but that didn't eliminate the order and structure that God had established for His people. That some leaders, even spiritual leaders, have abused their authority is undeniable. All too often, men and women have been appointed to spiritual leadership roles by people and institutions; but they lack the essential qualification of being called and appointed by God. Moses and Aaron weren't flawless, but they were established in their respective roles by God.

If we didn't know anything else about Moses, we could determine his heart and character by observing his response to the rebellion. Moses fell on his face and prayed to the Lord. (Numbers 16:4) Does that sound like a man who was arrogant or not called by God? And rather than lashing out against Korah and the others, Moses resolved to let God be his Defender. He didn't see the rebellion as a personal attack but said to them, "Therefore it is against the LORD that you and all your company have gathered together. What is Aaron that you grumble against him?" (Numbers 16:11) No angry tirades came from Moses or Aaron to defend their leadership or rehash all the ways that God had used them already.

If Korah and friends were in the right, then God would vindicate them. But Moses was secure in the truth that God had called him, and that God was leading him. "And Moses said, 'Hereby you shall know that the LORD has sent me to do all these works, and that it has not been of my own accord. If these men die as all men die, or if they are visited by the fate of all mankind, then the LORD has not sent me. But if the LORD creates something new, and the ground opens its mouth and swallows them up with all that belongs to them, and they go down alive into Sheol, then you shall know that these men have despised the LORD'" (Numbers 16:28–30). In case anyone had any lingering doubt or suspicion, the verdict came quickly. "And as soon as he had finished speaking all these words, the ground under them split apart. And the earth opened its mouth and swallowed them up, with their households and all the people who belonged to Korah and all their goods" (Numbers 16:31–32).

We probably shouldn't hold our breath for the ground to swallow up the next person who disagrees with us, but we can still learn from these events. What the New Testament establishes for the local church is different than the Old Testament, but God still appoints spiritual leaders. Korah's consequences do not, however, entail that we are never allowed to disagree with leadership or that accountability for leaders is inappropriate. We don't always have to agree, but we do need to honor the Lord and be genuinely humble. Pray more than you question. Encourage more than you complain.

Leadership in the church is a fearful and an awesome responsibility, a role that too many have not taken seriously enough. Many aspire to leadership roles, but a much smaller number aspire to be a servant of the Lord and His people. If your motivation and calling are to serve the Lord and His people, you don't even need a title, a position or an audience – just serve. Criticism and cynicism will always be easier than humble service. If God has called you to leadership, He will establish you in His plan and in His time. You won't need to undermine or overthrow anyone. Like Moses and others after him, serve the Lord with gladness in the place He has you today.

"For though the LORD is high, he regards the lowly,
but the haughty he knows from afar."
Psalm 138:6

HEAD TO HEART

- What do you think was really driving Korah and the others to rebel?

- Fair or unfair, how do you handle the criticism that comes your way?

- Why do you think God assigns people to different roles and responsibilities within the Body of Christ?

ACHAN: SIN IN THE CAMP

READING: JOSHUA 7

FOCUS: *Joshua 7:1 "But the people of Israel broke faith in regard to the devoted things, for Achan the son of Carmi, son of Zabdi, son of Zerah, of the tribe of Judah, took some of the devoted things. And the anger of the LORD burned against the people of Israel."*

On the heels of a glorious victory over Jericho, Joshua and the people of Israel were ready to continue the quest of claiming the land that God was giving to them. To occupy the land, they needed to drive out the Canaanites who were already living there. When the walls of Jericho came crashing down, the instructions for ransacking the city were clear. "And the city and all that is within it shall be devoted to the LORD for destruction" (Joshua 6:17a). But Achan took some of the devoted things for himself and stashed them, assuming no one would ever miss a few things here and there.

We know immediately what Joshua didn't: sin was in their camp, and God was more than slightly annoyed. The next battle should have been a small one. The scouting report on the city of Ai noted the people there were few and not even all the troops would be needed. Israel should make quick work of Ai and move on to the next conquest. Besides, who names their city using only two letters? But even without any consonants, Ai routed the attacking forces, and the people of Israel were suddenly devastated. An easy victory turned into a day of mourning. "And the hearts of the people melted and became as water. Then Joshua tore his clothes and fell to the earth on his face before the ark of the LORD until the evening, he and the elders of Israel. And they put dust on their heads" (Joshua 7:5b–6).

We can only imagine the anguish Joshua and the Israelites must have been experiencing. This was not how the conquest was supposed to go. If they couldn't even drive out Ai, they would have nothing but defeat moving forward. So Joshua sought the Lord, and the Lord answered him. "The LORD said to Joshua, 'Get up! Why have you fallen on your face? Israel has sinned; they have transgressed my covenant that I commanded them; they have taken some of the devoted things; they have stolen and lied and put them among their own belongings. Therefore the people of Israel cannot stand before their enemies. They turn their backs before their enemies, because they have become devoted for destruction. I will be with you no more, unless you destroy the devoted things from among you'" (Joshua 7:10–12).

Soon Achan was revealed as the perpetrator, and he confessed to the crime. "And Achan answered Joshua, 'Truly I have sinned against the LORD God of Israel, and this is what I did: when I saw among the spoil a beautiful cloak from Shinar, and 200 shekels of silver, and a bar of gold weighing 50 shekels, then I coveted them and took them. And see, they are hidden in the earth inside my tent, with the silver underneath'" (Joshua 7:20–21). Achan was quickly put to death because he had "transgressed the covenant of the LORD, and because he has done an outrageous thing in Israel" (Joshua 7:15b).

They dealt with the sin in the camp quickly and decisively – at least in part because God wanted them to see that one person's disobedience affected everyone. With the stench removed, God instructed Joshua to go up against Ai once again. Was Israel victorious over Ai this time? Aye!

As we consider what to glean from the story of Achan, caution and wisdom are needed. The lesson from Achan is not that we need to launch a witch hunt or conclude that everything bad that happens is the direct result of someone's hidden sin. But at the same time, we are foolish to assume that sin doesn't bring about serious consequences or that sins only affect the person who did the actual sinning.

In Achan's case, a battle was lost, men died and Israel was humiliated because one man decided to be greedy and disobedient. Yes, that was a unique situation and, of course, an example from the Old Testament; so it does not follow that someone will necessarily die as a result of our sin. Nevertheless, sin has a way of getting exposed to the light eventually. In unintended and unpredictable ways, our sin also affects those around us. So rather than asking ourselves who in our church or community might be living in sin, we might consider if we ourselves are capable of giving in to temptation the way that Achan did. Hint: the answer is yes.

Achan paid the price for his own sin, but Jesus has already paid the price for yours. Even if the consequences remain, there is no condemnation. (Romans 8:1) God sees and God knows; but we can walk in the light - not to get His forgiveness but because we already have His forgiveness.

> *"I acknowledged my sin to you, and I did not cover my iniquity;*
> *I said, 'I will confess my transgressions to the LORD,'*
> *and you forgave the iniquity of my sin."*
> Psalm 32:5

HEAD TO HEART

• How has your own sin affected other people?

• How should we handle situations of dealing with the sins of others?

• How does knowing that we are fully forgiven in Christ help us to walk in the light?

GIDEON: RIGHT ANSWER, WRONG MOTIVE

READING: JUDGES 8:22-27

FOCUS: *Judges 8:27 "And Gideon made an ephod of it and put it in his city, in Ophrah. And all Israel whored after it there, and it became a snare to Gideon and to his family."*

On the heels of great success for Gideon, the people of Israel wanted to make him their king. Since God had used him to overthrow the oppression of their enemies, who could be better than Gideon? They also offered to Gideon a dynasty as his offspring would continue to rule long after Gideon was dead. But Gideon gave the right answer: "I can't be your king because God is your King." The time was not right for a king in Israel; and even if the time had been right, Gideon was the wrong man. By all appearances, Gideon handled their request humbly and admirably; but sometimes ulterior motives lie beneath the right words.

Having declined the offer, what Gideon did next was bold – and tragic. Gideon immediately went on the take and took up a collection of golden earrings. He might as well have said, "I won't be your king, but I'll go ahead and help myself to your gold." Even though Gideon refused the title and responsibility of being the king, he did not refuse the privilege of receiving treasure from the people. He rejected the kingship with his words but then lived it up like a king with his actions. From Gideon's point of view, God could still be the King, but Gideon would be the treasurer.

But what did Gideon want with a pile of golden earrings? He apparently saw the need to fashion an idol. Using all the gold he collected, Gideon made a golden ephod. (An ephod was the chest piece worn by the high priest.) It is difficult to know exactly what Gideon was trying to do here; but his actions were foolish because, whatever Gideon's intentions were, the golden ephod became a snare to the people. The Bible is clear in saying that they whored after the golden idol. Gideon had led them right into sin.

Gideon may have been trying to establish himself as the mediator between God and the people while conveniently making his hometown the place to meet with God, but that was neither what God had wanted nor intended. Or worse, Gideon may have simply wanted the people to worship the golden object he had created. We would think that they would've remembered the last time someone made a golden image for the people to worship. Remember the golden calf? (Exodus 32) That didn't go very well either.

But Gideon wasn't finished. By the end of Judges 8, despite his lofty words, Gideon was living it up like a king. For example, he had 70 sons with numerous wives and a concubine at Shechem, which was excessive and reeking of self-importance. Eventually, Gideon sired another son with the concubine in Shechem and named him Abimelech, which just so happens to mean "my father is king." This speaks volumes about how Gideon viewed himself. He may not have been the king, but he thought of himself as a big deal.

We can easily recognize the wrongs of Gideon and the people of Israel here, but we often have trouble seeing our own. Many of us have learned all the verbiage to sound very "spiritual" as we seek to justify what we were planning to do anyway. We become experts at putting ourselves in the best light and rationalizing our decisions - whether we sought the Lord about them or not. Gideon looks to be sincere and certainly gives the right answer, but right answers without the right actions are useless. Time and circumstances have a way of demonstrating our true motivations - just as they did for Gideon. We can give all the right answers; but eventually, time will reveal our true motivations.

"Let the words of my mouth and the meditation of my heart
be acceptable in your sight, O LORD, my rock and my redeemer."
Psalm 19:14

HEAD TO HEART

- Have you seen others use "spiritual" words to essentially accomplish their own agendas?

- If God granted to you the measure of success that Gideon had experienced, do you think you would be able to handle it? In what ways would you be tempted?

- Someone has rightly said, "Time is on the side of truth." What will the passing of time demonstrate about your life?

ABIMELECH: SELFISH AMBITION

READING: JUDGES 9

FOCUS: *Judges 9:56 "Thus God returned the evil of Abimelech, which he committed against his father in killing his seventy brothers."*

Most people love a good story, especially when that story comes to a happy, satisfying conclusion. Even when the outcome is as predictable as a Hallmark Christmas movie, we like to see situations resolved with the bad guys losing and the good guys winning. If you love a glorious ending, you'll love the story of Abimelech. (Note: Abimelech is a common name in the Bible, so this is not the same Abimelech we see in the Abraham and Isaac stories).

Now, if Abimelech wasn't a good man, he came by that honestly. His father Gideon had glaring weaknesses that indirectly resulted in Abimelech being treated as an outcast among his own family. His half-brothers – all 70 of them – were born to Gideon's wives, whereas Abimelech's mother was a concubine Gideon had found in Shechem.

Unlike Gideon and the other judges, Abimelech was never called by God or even actually called one of the judges. Even so, Abimelech aspired to more than being one of Israel's judges. After Gideon's death, events quickly turned to Abimelech's plot to make himself the king. At least, the people had asked Gideon to rule. Abimelech was dangerously ambitious; but to become the king, he had to eliminate the other 70 rivals to the throne. Sadly, he nearly succeeded.

Judges 9:5 reads, "And he went to his father's house at Ophrah and killed his brothers the sons of Jerubbaal, seventy men, on one stone. But Jotham the youngest son of Jerubbaal was left, for he hid himself."

Thus, Abimelech elected himself as king. All the brothers - except for Jotham - were executed; and for some reason, Abimelech chose to kill them all on a single stone. Details are important.

Only Jotham remained to call out both Abimelech and those who had helped him gain power, and then Jotham ran for his life. Abimelech then ruled over Israel for the next three years. At this point in the story, we might start to wonder, "Where is God in all of this?" Sometimes God is quiet, but He is never absent.

Not surprisingly, Abimelech ruled as king in the same way he became the king, destroying anyone who happened to be in his way. Following in Gideon's own footsteps, Abimelech set out for personal vengeance against his enemies. On one occasion, Abimelech pursued his enemies into a tower and set a brushfire all around the tower. Over 1,000 people died in the flames as a result of his cruel vendetta; and for a time, Abimelech seemed to be getting away with more murder. Still out for vengeance, Abimelech then came to Thebez. Once again, the people there fled to a tower for refuge; and Abimelech began to employ the same brushfire strategy. "And Abimelech came to the tower and fought against it and drew near to the door of the tower to burn it with fire" (Judges 9:52).

Sometimes change can be a long time in coming but decisive and dramatic when the time finally arrives. A certain woman had fled to the tower at Thebez with all the others, but this woman had apparently brought along an upper millstone. We don't know why. Perhaps she always kept an extra upper millstone in her purse – *just in case*. And just like that: "And a certain woman threw an upper millstone on Abimelech's head and crushed his skull" (Judges 9:53).

Even with his skull cracked open (by a stone!), Abimelech was thinking only of himself to the very end - now concerned with his legacy. "Then he called quickly to the young man his armor-bearer and said to him, 'Draw your sword and kill me, lest they say of me, "A woman killed him."' And his young man thrust him through, and he died" (Judges 9:54). Even this scheme was ineffective. Years later, Abimelech's death by the hands of a woman was commonly known. (2 Samuel 11:21) Apparently, no one was overly saddened about Abimelech's demise either. "And when the men of Israel saw that Abimelech was dead, everyone departed to his home" (Judges 9:55). Abimelech was killed - now what's for dinner?

The narrator then assures us of God's involvement: "Thus God returned the evil of Abimelech, which he committed against his father in killing his seventy brothers" (Judges 9:56). While the story of Abimelech is an extreme example of selfish ambition, we all have the tendency to run over anyone or anything in our way. Instead of trying to run through a closed door, we need to wait in the assurance that God will bring us to the place He has prepared for us. The process will likely be slow and tedious, but God still opposes the proud and gives grace to the humble.

"The LORD lifts up the humble; he casts the wicked to the ground."
Psalm 147:6

HEAD TO HEART

- In what ways have your own ambitions been all about you instead of God?

- How can we seek to discern the difference between our plans and God's plans?

- Why does God seemingly allow evil to prosper for a time instead of crushing that evil ahead of time?

JEPHTHAH: MAKING A DEAL WITH GOD

READING: JUDGES 11

FOCUS: *Judges 11:30-31 "And Jephthah made a vow to the LORD and said, 'If you will give the Ammonites into my hand, then whatever comes out from the doors of my house to meet me when I return in peace from the Ammonites shall be the LORD's, and I will offer it up for a burnt offering.'"*

The story of Jephthah is one of the darkest and saddest stories in all the Bible. Even though the days of the judges in the Old Testament were never a spiritual highlight reel, the events of the story of Jephthah especially reflect just how dark the times had become.

Like his predecessor Abimelech, Jephthah knew the rejection of his own family as he was the son of a prostitute, while his half-brothers were born to his father's wife. Not surprisingly, they were less than accepting. But when the Ammonites made war against Israel, Jephthah, known as a mighty warrior, became necessary. "And they said to Jephthah, 'Come and be our leader, that we may fight against the Ammonites'" (Judges 11:6). While Jephthah agreed, the author of Judges never said that God called or raised up Jephthah for this role. But despite the appointment by man and despite what would happen next, the Spirit empowered Jephthah for battle. He was set up for success.

But Jephthah wanted to make a deal - not with those who put him in power and not even with the Ammonites. Instead Jephthah decided to make a deal with God. Jephthah prayed, "If you will give the Ammonites into my hand, then whatever comes out from the doors of my house to meet me when I return in peace from the Ammonites shall be the LORD's, and I will offer it up for a burnt offering" (Judges 11:30-31).

Rather than trusting God, Jephthah inexplicably thought he could bribe Him. This vow was nothing more than an attempt to secure God's help - not with an earnest request but with a quid pro quo. His vow was misguided, completely unnecessary and reflected a distorted view of God. Jephthah didn't grasp that he had no leverage with God and nothing to offer that God needed. God was going to do as He saw fit to do - with or without Jephthah's promise. "Our God is in the heavens; he does all that he pleases" (Psalm 115:3).

But Jephthah was indeed victorious and headed home to make good on his promise; after all, a deal is a deal. "Then Jephthah came to his home at Mizpah. And behold, his daughter came out to meet him with tambourines and with dances. She was his only child; besides her he had neither son nor daughter. And as soon as he saw her, he tore his clothes and said, 'Alas, my daughter! You have brought me very low, and you have become the cause of great trouble to me. For I have opened my mouth to the LORD, and I cannot take back my vow'" (Judges 11:34-35). Indeed, Jephthah was the one who had "opened his mouth"; while his daughter was noble and gracious and insisted that he must fulfill his vow to the Lord.

Did God want Jephthah to kill his daughter? Of course not. But Jephthah's resignation to carry out the promise betrayed his view of God as a tyrant who demanded bribes and was appeased by the sacrifice of His children. The story is so dark that some have denied that Jephthah truly carried out the vow and sacrificed his daughter, but the text simply does not allow this. "And at the end of two months, she returned to her father, who did with her according to his vow that he had made. She had never known a man, and it became a custom in Israel that the daughters of Israel went year by year to lament the daughter of Jephthah the Gileadite four days in the year"

(Judges 11:39-40). If that sounds horrible, it was.

Yes, Jephthah "did with her according to the vow he had made." But did the foolish vow have to be carried out? Generally, yes;, but in this case, no. First, the Old Testament Law *condemned* child sacrifice. (Deuteronomy 18:9–12) Also, Jephthah could have simply paid a temple tax and saved his daughter. (Leviticus 27:1-8) Viable loopholes already existed within the Law of Moses. If we ask why God didn't intervene, He already had intervened when He gave the Law. But even if Jephthah truly believed that he would be condemned by God for breaking the vow, he should have broken the vow, taking the wrath on himself instead of sacrificing his daughter.

Through this entire tragedy, may we be reminded that we don't ever need to bargain with God. His plan is better, and His heart towards His children is love. The sacrifice He desires is the *living* sacrifice of ourselves. (Romans 12:1-2) Even as we're disgusted and repulsed by Jephthah's horrific act, let's also remember that God sacrificed His only child but *willingly*. God's willingness to give His Son for us fully reveals His heart towards us. We have no need to wonder or waver. "What then shall we say to these things? If God is for us, who can be against us? He who did not spare his own Son but gave him up for us all, how will he not also with him graciously give us all things?" (Romans 8:31–32)

> *"The one who offers thanksgiving as his sacrifice glorifies me;*
> *to one who orders his way rightly I will show the salvation of God!"*
> Psalm 50:23

HEAD TO HEART

- Have you ever made a promise to God in an attempt to get a certain answer to prayer?

- How does our view of God shape the way that we pray?

- If God did not spare His only Son for us, why do we still doubt His heart towards us?

SAMSON: WHAT I WANT I WILL HAVE

READING: JUDGES 13-14

FOCUS: *Judges 14:3 "But his father and mother said to him, 'Is there not a woman among the daughters of your relatives, or among all our people, that you must go to take a wife from the uncircumcised Philistines?' But Samson said to his father, 'Get her for me, for she is right in my eyes.'"*

Maybe you remember growing up in Sunday School, learning about Samson and his mighty displays of strength. If significant details of his life are ignored, Samson could be considered the Bible's equivalent of a superhero. But most of the lessons from Samson's life warn us to go and do otherwise rather than go and do likewise. Samson entered the world as a special child with a calling to begin to deliver Israel from the Philistines; but when he grew up, Samson was on a different quest. The first words we hear from Samson's mouth reveal his focus and where his path will ultimately lead. "Then he came up and told his father and mother, 'I saw one of the daughters of the Philistines at Timnah. Now get her for me as my wife'" (Judges 14:2).

This woman was not even the infamous Delilah, but these words mark the beginning of a pattern of disobedience repeated throughout Samson's life. Maybe Philistine women really were that attractive, but the Philistines also happened to be the enemy. Samson's calling from God to begin to deliver Israel from the Philistines would be especially challenging if Samson were married to one of their daughters. Imagine the awkward conversations that would occur at family gatherings. But

Samson demanded the woman because she was right in his eyes. In a great irony, the day would come when Samson would lose his eyes; but long before that, Samson was already blinded by his own desires. He was ignoring the things he desperately needed to see.

First, Samson ignored his **calling**. Why? Because he wanted her; and in his mind, he should have her. "Now get her for me as my wife." But before Samson even saw the woman, he had already put himself in a place where he should not have been. What was he doing in one of the Philistine cities anyway? By going there, he was already giving ground to the enemy. From Samson, we glean this warning: *don't flirt with what can destroy you.* We face enough temptations already - don't put yourself in a position that makes giving in easier.

Secondly, Samson ignored wise **counsel**. Of course, he wasn't the first and wouldn't be the last. Samson's parents tried to talk some sense into him. "But Samson, she's on the other team!" While Samson may or may not have been the last young person to disregard parental advice, his response was harsh and reeked of entitlement: "Get her for me, for she is right in my eyes."

Clearly Samson was foolish, but who do you have in your own life that can tell you when you're wrong? Do you seek out wise counsel, or do you determine all your steps? We all need outside wisdom because we can be easily deceived. Unlike Samson, *don't disregard the ones who are trying to help you.* If you have people in your life who are willing to question your decisions and attitudes, listen to them. If you don't, seek them out.

Finally, Samson ignored the potential **consequences**. We aren't surprised that this relationship with the Philistine woman didn't last. Samson discovered that, in addition to being the enemy, the Philistines were less than trustworthy - who knew? All the while, Samson seemingly never considered how his choices could bring disaster. May we learn the lesson that Samson apparently never did: *don't follow what will* *mislead you.* No matter how important it seems right now, have you considered the potential consequences? Ignoring them led to Samson's inglorious end.

Is there any good news in all of this? Even while Samson was making a mess of things, God was still ruling over the universe and had never relinquished His control. Samson's choices didn't take God by surprise, and his failures didn't alter God's plan. Samson's parents were right to seek to correct him, but there was something they could not have known. "His father and mother did not know that it was from the LORD, for he was seeking an opportunity against the Philistines. At that time the Philistines ruled over Israel" (Judges 14:4).

Despite all that was wrong, we can be comforted by Samson's story. Many of us have done our very best to ruin our lives with our bad choices and their consequences. But God's sovereignty has already taken into consideration our choices, and God still accomplishes His purposes. We've certainly tried, but we don't have the power to ruin everything. Whether Samson was in line with God's purposes or not, God could still use him. And God can still use you.

"For you, O Lord, are my hope, my trust, O LORD, from my youth.
Upon you I have leaned from before my birth; you are he who took me
from my mother's womb. My praise is continually of you."
Psalm 71:5–6

HEAD TO HEART

- Why do you think great weaknesses tend to accompany great strengths and abilities?

- In what ways have you been blinded by sinful desires?

- Why would God choose to work through Samson's bad choices instead of preventing him from making them in the first place?

SAMSON: RUNNING AWAY FROM GRACE

READING: JUDGES 14-15

FOCUS: *Judges 15:18-19a "And he was very thirsty, and he called upon the LORD and said, 'You have granted this great salvation by the hand of your servant, and shall I now die of thirst and fall into the hands of the uncircumcised?' And God split open the hollow place that is at Lehi, and water came out from it. And when he drank, his spirit returned, and he revived."*

Even before Samson was born, the Angel of the Lord appeared to his parents with specific instructions for his upbringing. Samson was a special person with a special calling, and this required him to be set apart. He was never supposed to be like everyone else. In the same way, you have probably discovered that you can't follow Jesus while at the same time being like everyone else. As an evidence of Samson's special calling, he was set apart from birth as a Nazirite. (Judges 13:5) One of the provisions of the Nazirite vow required that no razor would touch Samson's head. Ultimately, Samson would surrender this secret and relinquish the only remaining aspect of what had set him apart.

But the haircut was just the final straw. The Nazirite vow had *three* requirements, not one. Besides not letting a razor touch his head, the Nazirite vow also required that Samson avoid grapes and from going near a dead body. (Numbers 6) These requirements might seem random and rigid to us; but for Samson, they were the special requirements for a person with both a high calling and extraordinary abilities. What was required of Samson was comparatively small in the light of the abilities that God had granted him and what God had called him to do.

Even as Samson was displaying astonishing feats of strength, he was also forfeiting his calling. The first two violations are more subtle than the last, but they were key factors. First, Samson did not avoid grapes. The Bible doesn't directly state that Samson consumed wine but provides a specific clue. If Samson had ever been able to show restraint in other areas, we might give him the benefit of the doubt, but Samson's ongoing lifestyle prevents that. "Then Samson went down with his father and mother to Timnah, and they came to the vineyards of Timnah" (Judges 14:5a). This was more than a nice family outing and, in the context of the rest of the story, raises the suspicion that Samson had been there before. The clue is the mention of the vineyards. If the narrator was not intending to tell us something, why even mention the vineyards? Strike one.

The second violation was more evident in that Samson clearly did not avoid the carcass of a dead animal. When a young, roaring lion charged at Samson, he was not in the wrong to defend himself and kill the lion (with his bare hands!). But later Samson stopped to see the carcass which, by then, had a beehive inside; and the rotting carcass was now full of honey. True to form, Samson wanted the honey, so he would have the honey. "He scraped it out into his hands and went on, eating as he went. And he came to his father and mother and gave some to them, and they ate. But he did not tell them that he had scraped the honey from the carcass of the lion" (Judges 14:9). Funny that Samson didn't mention where he found the honey. We could say that what Samson did was a "gross violation" of the second portion of the vow. Strike two.

To his credit, Samson did make life miserable for the Philistines. His supernatural strength was on full display on several occasions, but the victories over the Philistines seemed only to reinforce his confidence in himself instead of a humble reliance on the Lord. But then Samson had a real moment of crisis. One of the better-known incidents of Samson's life occurred when he killed 1,000 Philistines with the "fresh jawbone" of a donkey. While this was an astonishing feat, the narrator may have been implying that Samson had again touched a dead body. In any event, Samson was famished and feared dying of thirst. But amazingly, Samson cried out to the Lord. "You have granted this great salvation by the hand of your servant, and shall I now die of thirst and fall into the hands of the uncircumcised?" (Judges 15:18b)

This is the first time in Scripture that Samson ever cried out to God, and God responded with grace. God miraculously provided for Samson, and he was revived. For all that Samson had failed to be - up until this point, God gave him an opportunity. This could have been the turning point at which Samson finally recognized God's hand in his life and moved towards fulfilling God's special calling. Like Samson, we can respond in one of two ways to God's grace. We can turn away from sin, or we can keep running to sin because we think we got away with it.

Now you probably don't remember the last time you nearly died after killing 1,000 Philistines with a jawbone, but you may have had some moments where God brought you to the end of yourself. God surely gives second chances. God shows mercy and grace. God pursues us when we aren't giving Him a thought. He is a God of grace, but He will not be mocked. He owes none of us more chances.

If you've got some Samson in you, this is the time to break the cycle. Stop doing what you've done every time before, and trust God. This is the time to repent and return. Don't run away from grace.

If we wondered how Samson would respond to the grace of God, we don't have to wonder long. The next verse tells us, but the news isn't good. At some point later, "Samson went to Gaza, and there he saw a prostitute, and he went in to her" (Judges 16:1). Strike three was just a matter of time. This was the beginning of the end for Samson, but how will you respond to God's grace?

"Seek the LORD while he may be found; call upon him while he is near
let the wicked forsake his way, and the unrighteous man his thoughts;
let him return to the LORD, that he may have compassion on him,
and to our God, for he will abundantly pardon."
Isaiah 55:6-7

HEAD TO HEART

• In what ways do you live by different standards because of your relationship with God?

• What causes people to seem to be determined to destroy themselves and their purpose?

• What has God's grace done in your life?

ELI: RAISING 'EM WRONG

READING: 1 SAMUEL 3

FOCUS: *1 Samuel 3:13 "And I declare to him that I am about to punish his house forever, for the iniquity that he knew, because his sons were blaspheming God, and he did not restrain them."*

One of the saddest situations we encounter in this life is when a child is raised to fear God and love God but later walks away from his or her faith. Whether they are off in the far country for only a season or if they never return, the child leaves their parents with immeasurable grief. As parents, we do our best to raise our children well; but they ultimately belong to the Lord. As God has entrusted the raising of His children to us as parents, one of the words we must learn to use is "no." God is our perfect heavenly Father. And yet, He has no difficulty in telling us no or, even worse, wait. "No" doesn't help us win Parent of the Year awards or elicit delighted responses, but we can't parent effectively without it.

Since the only ones who have not made parenting mistakes are not parents yet, we are wise to avoid jumping to hasty conclusions about others' parenting skills or their lack of parenting skills. But there is one situation we know about for sure. We know precisely why the kids turned out badly because the Bible tells us. When the Bible first introduces us to the sons of Eli the priest, before we're even told their names, we learn that they were worthless and that they did not know the Lord. Not knowing the Lord and being generally worthless is problematic enough, but Hophni and Phinehas were also "serving" in the temple.

"Now Eli was very old, and he kept hearing all that his sons were doing to all Israel, and how they lay with the women who were serving at the entrance to the tent of meeting. And he said to them, 'Why do you do such things? For I hear of your evil dealings from all these people'" (1 Samuel 2:22–23). No wonder Eli was upset – his sons were using the temple of the Lord as a brothel. At least at this point, Eli scolded his sons; but by the time all this was occurring, Eli's words were empty and falling on deaf ears. After Eli's rebuke, the narrator ominously adds, "But they would not listen to the voice of their father, for it was the will of the LORD to put them to death" (1 Samuel 2:25b). Notice it wasn't that they wouldn't listen, so God decided to put them to death. Instead God already had decided to put them to death, so they wouldn't listen. By then, it was apparently too late for Eli's wicked sons.

Soon a prophet revealed to Eli that judgment was coming on his household and that his sons would die on the same day. But how did the situation reach this point? Why had God already determined to put the worthless sons to death so that they would not listen to their father? Ironically, we are given more details from the Word of the Lord to the young boy Samuel whom Eli affectionately referred to as "my son." When Samuel finally said to the Lord, "Speak, for your servant hears," God revealed to Samuel that He was about to bring judgment on the house of Eli. His words are particularly telling: "And I declare to him that I am about to punish his house forever, for the iniquity that he knew, because his sons were blaspheming God, and he did not restrain them" (1 Samuel 3:13). Eli's failure was that he had known what his sons were doing, and he failed to restrain them.

Perhaps it all started with much smaller issues. Eli should have said "no" to his boys but didn't. When their reckless behavior carried over into the temple service, Eli should have stepped in to correct or remove them; but apparently, he didn't. By the time their actions had escalated to blasphemy, sacrilege, immorality and all within the temple, Hophni and Phinehas had forfeited their opportunity to walk the aisle and rededicate their lives at the next revival service. Yes, Hophni and

Phinehas were worthless men; but they had help getting there. Eli knew what was happening and shirked the responsibility of correcting his sons. Not long after, the Ark of the Covenant was captured by the Philistines; Hophni and Phinehas died in battle; and Eli died rather ingloriously - all on the same day. Thankfully at the same time, God was raising up the prophet Samuel who would be a man of God for all of his days.

Eli's story is more than a clinic in poor parenting - although his example certainly was that. We can learn from Eli's failure. In the areas that God has given us responsibility, are we seeing evil and choosing to look the other way? Are we choosing to take the easy road of indifference when we need to walk the much steeper path of confrontation? We would not be the first to be unpopular for taking a stand for righteousness, but taking a little criticism is better than gradually ending up like Eli. We aren't responsible for all the evil that goes on in the world, but we are accountable for the areas that God has entrusted to us. Hophni and Phinehas may have still become worthless, but Eli squandered the opportunity to do what was right. May we never dishonor the Lord in what we allow or tolerate.

> *"Mark the blameless and behold the upright,*
> *for there is a future for the man of peace.*
> *But transgressors shall be altogether destroyed;*
> *the future of the wicked shall be cut off."*
> Psalm 37:37–38

HEAD TO HEART

- How much of the blame goes to Eli, and how much goes to his sons for their evil?

- What are some of the risks we take in seeking to confront sinful actions or attitudes?

- How do we discern the right time and right way to speak out against evil?

SAUL: CHARACTER COUNTS

READING: 1 SAMUEL 13

FOCUS: *1 Samuel 13:8–9 "He waited seven days, the time appointed by Samuel. But Samuel did not come to Gilgal, and the people were scattering from him. So Saul said, 'Bring the burnt offering here to me, and the peace offerings.' And he offered the burnt offering."*

Israel had decided that the time had come for a king, dismissing Samuel's answer that God was already their King. Not only was the timing of the request wrong, but the deeper issue was the motivation behind the request. Israel wanted a king because the other nations had kings. You may remember your attempts to reason with your parents that you should have something because someone you knew already had one. How did any of us survive such injustice? Essentially, Israel was making the same argument in wanting a king – but *they* have one! Ultimately, God gave Israel a king but not without warning them that this wouldn't go well.

When Saul was selected and introduced to the people, he looked the part and met their criteria. What qualified Saul to be the king? He was tall. And for good measure, handsome as well. "There was not a man among the people of Israel more handsome than he. From his shoulders upward he was taller than any of the people" (1 Samuel 9:2b). No wonder they were so enamored with their new king.

But God was gracious and gave King Saul the opportunity to succeed. Samuel warned the people of Israel, "Only fear the LORD and serve him faithfully with all your heart. For consider what great things he has done for you. But if you still do wickedly, you shall be swept away, both you and your king" (1 Samuel 12:24–25). King Saul started out with a measure of humility and won a victory over one of Israel's enemies, but soon the challenges of being the king would reveal that Saul's heart and character fell short of his stature.

Samuel was undoubtedly the prophet of the Lord of his day, and his instructions to Saul were clear. "Then go down before me to Gilgal. And behold, I am coming down to you to offer burnt offerings and to sacrifice peace offerings. Seven days you shall wait, until I come to you and show you what you shall do" (1 Samuel 10:8). These instructions might have seemed easy enough at the time, but following them under duress proved to be a tall order – even for Saul.

The Philistines were threatening, and the people of Israel were fearful. As they assembled at Gilgal, Saul waited for Samuel - and waited some more. The seventh day arrived, but Samuel hadn't. "He waited seven days, the time appointed by Samuel. But Samuel did not come to Gilgal, and the people were scattering from him. So Saul said, 'Bring the burnt offering here to me, and the peace offerings.' And he offered the burnt offering" (1 Samuel 13:8–9). Almost on cue, Samuel finally arrived as Saul was standing there by the fire for the offering he should not have made. Samuel arrived on, not before, the seventh day; but Saul hadn't waited. Like a parent interrogating a child, Samuel asked, "What have you done?"

Saul's answer to Samuel was more revealing than he realized. "When I saw that the people were scattering from me, and that you did not come within the days appointed, and that the Philistines had mustered at Michmash, I said, 'Now the Philistines will come down against me at Gilgal, and I have not sought the favor of the LORD.' So I forced myself, and offered the burnt offering" (1 Samuel 13:11b-12). What could have been an opportunity for Saul to stand strong ended up being the circumstance that exposed him. Saul's heart was motivated by popularity, self-preservation and the need for approval, resulting in his attempt to control the outcome. Saul hadn't been forced to do anything; he simply acted in his own behalf. If a leader frets every time the people begin to scatter (or disagree or criticize), he or she will either cease being a leader or become irrelevant and ineffective. In time, Saul would do both.

Saul disobeyed the Word of the Lord; so he could save face, and the consequences were severe. Saul's "dynasty" would end with Saul; his sons would not succeed him. God was seeking out a man after His own heart (1 Samuel 13:14), and Saul had demonstrated that he was not that man. Dire circumstances don't give us the option to ignore God's commands and do as we see fit. We might be tempted to think that Saul's punishment was severe, but God knew this was only the beginning. Making the sacrifice himself established a pattern of disobedience in Saul's life that continued to escalate until the bitter end. Sometimes obedience is costly, difficult and terribly inconvenient; but never assume that disobedience is free. On this side of the cross, we are fully accepted and forgiven in Jesus; but our choices still matter and our character counts. Trust God enough to humbly obey His commandments. He hasn't been wrong yet.

"And I will give you a new heart,
and a new spirit I will put within you.
And I will remove the heart of stone from your flesh
and give you a heart of flesh. And I will put my Spirit within you,
and cause you to walk in my statutes
and be careful to obey my rules."
Ezekiel 36:26–27

HEAD TO HEART

• Why couldn't Samuel have arrived before the seventh day? What would have been different?

• What were Saul's real motivations when he chose to not wait for Samuel?

- In what areas do you struggle to obey God? What makes these things difficult?

SAUL: PARTIAL OBEDIENCE

READING: 1 SAMUEL 15

FOCUS: *1 Samuel 15:9 "But Saul and the people spared Agag and the best of the sheep and of the oxen and of the fattened calves and the lambs, and all that was good, and would not utterly destroy them. All that was despised and worthless they devoted to destruction."*

Some words have various meanings or nuances of meaning that can lead to misinterpretation or misunderstanding. However, the word "all" leaves no room for confusion. When God spoke to Saul through the prophet Samuel, the instructions He gave were for Saul to go and destroy all the Amalekites and devote to destruction all that they had. (1 Samuel 15:1-3) Whether the task itself was difficult to accomplish or not, the directive was clear.

Saul went on to engage the Amalekites in battle and was victorious. So far, so good. But remember the part about "all"? "But Saul and the people spared Agag and the best of the sheep and of the oxen and of the fattened calves and the lambs, and all that was good, and would not utterly destroy them. All that was despised and worthless they devoted to destruction" (1 Samuel 15:9). If all the Amalekites were to be destroyed, wouldn't that especially apply to their king? But Saul and the people spared Agag and all the good livestock. They destroyed the rest, so Saul carried out God's command – mostly.

Was Saul's obedience good enough? Did close count? We don't have to wonder long. "The word of the LORD came to Samuel: 'I regret that I have made Saul king, for he has turned back from following me and has not performed my commandments.' And Samuel was angry, and he cried to the LORD all night" (1 Samuel 15:10–11). Now Saul didn't know this; and when Samuel came to Saul the next day, Saul was ready to tell Samuel all about his glorious victory. "Blessed be you to the LORD. I have performed the commandment of the LORD" (1 Samuel 15:13b). Did Saul really think he had been truly obedient? Was he unclear on the concept of "all"?

"And Samuel said, 'What then is this bleating of the sheep in my ears and the lowing of the oxen that I hear?'" (1 Samuel 15:14) Saul, if you obeyed God's command, why all the mooing? At this point, we don't know if Saul had already practiced his answer or if he was just quick-thinking to come up with his excuse. "Saul said, 'They have brought them from the Amalekites, for the people spared the best of the sheep and of the oxen to sacrifice to the LORD your God, and the rest we have devoted to destruction'" (1 Samuel 15:15). We saved the best of the livestock to . . . um . . . well . . . to sacrifice them to the Lord! Yeah, they're all for the Lord. Nice try, but Samuel wasn't buying it.

Samuel demanded to know, "Why then did you not obey the voice of the LORD? Why did you pounce on the spoil and do what was evil in the sight of the LORD?" (1 Samuel 15:19) Saul's partial obedience was just another form of disobedience. When Saul continued to defend his actions and defer blame to the people, Samuel spoke these well-known words: "Has the LORD as great delight in burnt offerings and sacrifices, as in obeying the voice of the LORD? Behold, to obey is better than sacrifice, and to listen than the fat of rams. For rebellion is as the sin of divination, and presumption is as iniquity and idolatry. Because you have rejected the word of the LORD, he has also rejected you from being king" (1 Samuel 15:22b–23).

God didn't want a sacrifice; He wanted obedience. Saul finally confessed his wrongdoing and even admitted what had brought about his failure. "Saul said to Samuel, 'I have sinned, for I have transgressed the commandment of the LORD and your words, because I feared the people and obeyed their voice'" (1 Samuel 15:24). Once again,

Saul valued the affirmation and approval from people to the point of being disobedient to the Lord. Even after coming clean, Saul was still wanting to save face in the sight of the people. Saul said to Samuel, "I have sinned; yet honor me now before the elders of my people and before Israel, and return with me, that I may bow before the LORD your God" (1 Samuel 15:30). "I have sinned" and "honor me now" simply don't go well together. Saul would continue as king for a while longer; but having now been rejected by the Lord, Saul became the ultimate lame duck. The new king would be anointed - even as Saul still held the title. King Agag didn't fare any better when Samuel hacked him into pieces.

Since Jesus was the final, ultimate sacrifice, today we don't offer sacrifices; and yet we can still attempt to substitute worship for obedience. Worship music has become so popular in our modern church culture, but are we singing God another song without offering Him the sacrifice of our obedience? Yes, it's so much easier to sing the song than live the life; but the lyrics of the most worshipful song we sing are empty words if they don't reflect how we live. Authentic worship is offered more in how we live moment by moment than in the songs we sing in a worship gathering. To obey is still better than sacrifice.

"The sacrifices of God are a broken spirit; a broken and contrite heart,
O God, you will not despise."
Psalm 51:17

HEAD TO HEART

- What motivated Saul and the people to spare the king and the good livestock?

- In what ways are we tempted to substitute worship or service in the place of obedience?

- Is there any area of your life in which you might be rejecting the word of the Lord?

NABAL: NOBODY'S FOOL

READING: 1 SAMUEL 25

FOCUS: *1 Samuel 25:17b ". . . and he is such a worthless man that one cannot speak to him."*

From an outsider's perspective, Nabal had a lot of things going for him. He was not only wealthy but had a wise and beautiful wife. However, anyone who knew him was evidently aware that Nabal was also a fool. That may sound harsh, but that's what his name meant - fool. That was probably not his *given* name - unless his parents had a mean streak, but Nabal often succeeded in living up to his name. Sometimes we hear that opposites attract, which might have been true in the case of Nabal and his wife Abigail. Where she was discerning and beautiful, Nabal was "harsh and badly behaved" (1 Samuel 25:3b). You may already have thought of someone who might be a direct descendant of Nabal.

As the story unfolds, David and his men were passing through and humbly asked Nabal for provisions. The text reveals that David wasn't trying to take advantage but only to receive whatever Nabal could spare. Had Nabal politely declined the request, the situation probably would not have escalated. But Nabal was compelled to be foolish and thus reacted harshly and insultingly to David. David's response was clear: "Every man strap on his sword!" and 400 of David's men were ready to rumble.

As the tensions were building, one of Nabal's servants went to Abigail to tell her what was about to happen. The servant's words are telling. "Now therefore know this and consider what you should do, for harm is determined against our master and against all his house, and he is such a worthless man that one cannot speak to him" (1 Samuel 25:17).

The servant must have known that he could speak freely to Abigail concerning her husband, so evidently Nabal's foolishness was no secret. Nabal's actions were now endangering everyone, but no one could speak to him because they knew he wouldn't listen. As the expression goes: "You couldn't tell him nothing!" What the expression lacks in grammar, it makes up for in accuracy.

David was a warrior and was prepared to handle Nabal decisively; but in her wisdom, Abigail was able to reason with David. "Let not my lord regard this worthless fellow, Nabal, for as his name is, so is he. Nabal is his name, and folly is with him" (1 Samuel 25:25a). Abigail spoke a harsh truth, but she was right. Abigail further encouraged David to let God handle the situation, and David saw the wisdom in her words. "And David said to Abigail, 'Blessed be the LORD, the God of Israel, who sent you this day to meet me! Blessed be your discretion, and blessed be you, who have kept me this day from bloodguilt and from working salvation with my own hand!'" (1 Samuel 25:32–33)

David wisely backed off and let God be his Defender. We've seen situations that take a long time to be resolved, but God handled this situation rather quickly. "And Abigail came to Nabal, and behold, he was holding a feast in his house, like the feast of a king. And Nabal's heart was merry within him, for he was very drunk. So she told him nothing at all until the morning light. In the morning, when the wine had gone out of Nabal, his wife told him these things, and his heart died within him, and he became as a stone. And about ten days later the LORD struck Nabal, and he died" (1 Samuel 25:36–38). God indeed handled the situation.

When we consider what to glean from the story of Nabal, the "low-hanging fruit" is obviously to avoid being a fool like Nabal and to never be the person who can't be told anything. If that is you, stop that right now. But hopefully you aren't that person; and if you were, no one could tell you that anyway. Ideally, we're all closer to the wise end of the spectrum; but that doesn't insulate us from having to deal with those who must have descended from Nabal and walk the earth today. Oh, how they are among us!

Abigail had words of wisdom for David that very much apply for us as well. Like David, we're wise to let God handle the modern-day Nabals. We can and probably have responded in kind, but that accomplishes nothing. Instead we treat them with kindness and don't allow ourselves to be brought to their level, remembering that we too have acted foolishly on occasion. God handled Nabal then, and He continues to handle those who walk in foolishness today. We don't have to fight on our own behalf as we are fully assured that God will fight for us.

"He who is often reproved, yet stiffens his neck,
will suddenly be broken beyond healing."
Proverbs 29:1

HEAD TO HEART

- In what ways have you possibly or definitely acted like Nabal?

- How do you typically respond when you encounter someone who reminds you of Nabal?

- Why is it best to let God handle the situation instead of fighting the battle ourselves?

DAVID: DON'T FOLLOW YOUR HEART

READING: 1 SAMUEL 27:1-8

FOCUS: *1 Samuel 27:1 "Then David said in his heart, 'Now I shall perish one day by the hand of Saul. There is nothing better for me than that I should escape to the land of the Philistines. Then Saul will despair of seeking me any longer within the borders of Israel, and I shall escape out of his hand.'"*

King David is one of the most loved and celebrated characters in all of Scripture, but his feet of clay were revealed through his sandals more than once. David's most famous failure was, of course, the Bathsheba debacle (2 Samuel 11-12); but that was not his first rodeo in failure. Back when King David was just David, he nearly jeopardized God's plan for Israel and the fulfillment of God's promise. Out of fatigue and desperation, David reached a decision that could have prevented him from ever becoming the king.

To be fair, David hadn't arrived at this place of despair without help. The path he had traveled up to this point was long and difficult; and from where he stood, the glorious ending was still nowhere in sight. When the shepherd boy was called in from the field to be anointed as the new king of Israel, he likely had no idea that his new journey would be so long and life-threatening. Having already killed Goliath the Philistine and having fought other battles against the Philistines, David now decided that his circumstances had become so bleak that the only thing left for him to do was to flee to the Philistines.

David had understandably grown weary of running for his life. As 1 Samuel 19-26 details, Saul's attempts to kill David continued as Saul grew increasingly jealous and paranoid. That David was on the way up and Saul was on the way down were evident - but especially so to Saul. When he heard the women singing, "Saul has struck down his thousands, and David his *tens of thousands*," he raged with jealousy and set out to eliminate David.

While we understand that Saul was on the brink of insanity, we might wonder why God would allow him to continue and not immediately put an end to Saul's evil. The inconvenient truth is that God was allowing all of this to grow and prepare David. God didn't command Saul to pursue or kill David, but that was His process of preparation for David. Even now, God's ways of preparing and refining us are neither what we would expect nor choose; but we trust that He knows what He's doing.

Even as Saul pursued him, David had the opportunity to kill Saul, get his revenge and assume the kingship (twice!); but he refused to harm God's anointed. (1 Samuel 24, 26) The restraint David showed on those occasions was astounding. He was clearly winning this battle, and King Saul himself knew that David would soon become the king.

But then it happened. "Then David said in his heart. . . ." David reached the point of exhaustion and began talking to himself in his heart. Worse than that, he started *listening* to his heart. Notice the Bible does not say that David sought the Lord or wise counsel; he just followed his heart. "Just follow your heart" was a terrible idea then, and this tidbit of sloganized nonsense is especially prevalent today. You don't want to follow your heart; you want to follow God's Word. As Jeremiah 17:9 says, "The heart is deceitful above all things, and desperately sick; who can understand it?" You can't trust your heart, so why follow it? This is why knowing Scripture is essential. Our hearts, our feelings and often even our minds are bad gauges; but the Word of God tells us the truth.

David obviously knew "the Lord is my Shepherd"; but in the moment, he had forgotten. At the point when he needed them the most, David stopped reminding himself of God's promises. Then the lies emerged to fill the void. "Now I shall perish one day by the hand of Saul" (1 Samuel 27:1a). Was God's protection of David going to finally run out? "There is nothing better for me than that I should escape to the land of the Philistines" (1 Samuel 27:1a). No, David, what you could do is continue to trust the Lord. As David's story reveals, when we're exhausted and don't know what to do, we're especially vulnerable to following our own hearts right into disaster.

"And when it was told Saul that David had fled to Gath, he no longer sought him" (1 Samuel 27:4). Problem solved, right? Perhaps temporarily, but nothing good came out of David's time with the Philistines; and he nearly crossed the line of fighting against Israel, a potentially tragic and irreversible move. But in time and through catastrophic events, God mercifully recaptured David's focus and restored David to Himself. (1 Samuel 30)

Perhaps you can relate to David in having to walk a long and difficult road. From your current point of view, maybe no end is in sight. But keep trusting, keep waiting, keep worshipping. Yes, the road has been long and hard; but be assured in your heart - there's nothing for you in the land of the Philistines.

> *"Wait for the LORD; be strong,*
> *and let your heart take courage; wait for the LORD!"*
> Psalm 27:14

HEAD TO HEART

- In what ways are you tempted to give in or give up when your life is difficult?

- What can you do to make sure that you don't go to "the land of the Philistines"?

- What promises of God help you remain right where God has called you to be?

ABSALOM: UNDERMINING FOR GOLD

READING: 2 SAMUEL 15, 18

FOCUS: *2 Samuel 15:3–4 "Absalom would say to him, 'See, your claims are good and right, but there is no man designated by the king to hear you.' Then Absalom would say, 'Oh that I were judge in the land! Then every man with a dispute or cause might come to me, and I would give him justice.'"*

As difficult as this may be to accept, throughout history, certain politicians have been less than honest and have not always had the purest of motives in seeking office or remaining there. Sometimes we act as though the corrupt politician was invented within our lifetime, but corruption predates even politics.

We remember that King David made some exceptionally bad, life-altering choices. (2 Samuel 11) The forgiveness and restoration that God afforded to David did not remove the consequences that David's actions set in motion. Nathan the prophet told the truth: the sword would never depart from David's house. In the same way, God loves us, and God forgives us; but in the world He created, what we cause inevitably has effects.

Following a recurring Old Testament trend, Absalom decided that he should be the king of Israel. This desire might have been a noble ambition if Israel didn't already have a king and if that king wasn't Absalom's father David. To further complicate the situation, despite his failures, David was God's anointed king. But families are complicated, and David's family was especially so. Rape and murder within the family had already occurred (2 Samuel 13), but the saga would now turn to insurrection. Absalom knew the only pathway to his kingship was by eliminating his father, but that was a price he was willing to pay. Let the political circus begin.

Before we consider what Absalom did, let's consider how he was able to do it. "Now in all Israel there was no one so much to be praised for his handsome appearance as Absalom. From the sole of his foot to the crown of his head there was no blemish in him. And when he cut the hair of his head (for at the end of every year he used to cut it; when it was heavy on him, he cut it), he weighed the hair of his head, two hundred shekels by the king's weight" (2 Samuel 14:25–26). Like King Saul before him, Absalom looked the part of the king. He was handsome and had a mane that would make a lion jealous. People have been getting ahead solely based on their outward appearance for a long time now.

In addition to his looks, Absalom was a schemer and a manipulator, who knew how to work a crowd. Absalom would stand at the gate of the city, intercepting those who were seeking an audience with the king. "Absalom would say to him, 'See, your claims are good and right, but there is no man designated by the king to hear you.' Then Absalom would say, 'Oh that I were judge in the land! Then every man with a dispute or cause might come to me, and I would give him justice'" (2 Samuel 15:3–4). Yes, Absalom was so deeply concerned about the common man. He felt their pain. And over time, Absalom's scheming was effective. "So Absalom stole the hearts of the men of Israel" (2 Samuel 15:6b). He surely had them fooled. With that, Absalom had started the rebellion to overthrow the king.

Once the rebellion was in full swing, David had to flee Jerusalem since his kingdom had been overthrown by his son. While Absalom was responsible and accountable for his actions, David knew this was another evidence of the sword never departing from his house. Perhaps Absalom would have been a better leader. Maybe David's personal life had become too much of a distraction. But all political considerations aside, David remained God's anointed, making Absalom's rebellion ultimately against God's rule - not David's. In stark contrast, David had refused to harm King Saul when he could have - not because Saul was in the right but because Saul was God's anointed.

The insurrection was a tumultuous time for Israel but relatively short-lived. The very symbol of Absalom's appeal became his downfall when the beautiful mane got caught in some tree branches. Absalom was helplessly suspended above the ground, hanging by his own hair and giving new meaning to having a "bad hair day." David's men finished him off quickly, ending the rebellion but causing deep sadness for David in the death of his son. (2 Samuel 18)

Today we don't have kings, but we do have leaders - some called by God and some not. Are they always right? Not at all. Are they above being questioned? Never. Sometimes we disagree with those in leadership, and our disagreement with leadership does not make us automatically wrong or entail that we have an "authority problem." But especially in a spiritual setting, we cannot become an Absalom. When you can no longer be supportive, the time may have come to quietly and graciously walk away. Where "Absaloms" undermine and foment cynicism, "Davids" yield to God's authority - even in disagreement. Yes, these issues require grace and wisdom; but God will supply them as we yield ourselves to His rule and authority.

> *"Wait for the LORD and keep his way, and he will exalt you to inherit the land; you will look on when the wicked are cut off."*
> Psalm 37:34

HEAD TO HEART

- How do you guard against cynicism and a critical spirit when you disagree with a leader?

- What do you think motivated Absalom to rebel? Anger? Greed? Selfish ambition?

- Do you pray for those in leadership, especially in positions of spiritual leadership?

REHOBOAM: THE COMPANION OF FOOLS

READING: 1 KINGS 12:1-24

FOCUS: *1 Kings 12:8 "But he abandoned the counsel that the old men gave him and took counsel with the young men who had grown up with him and stood before him."*

With all the wisdom that God had invested in Solomon, we might assume that the son of Solomon would have inherited at least some of that wisdom. But Rehoboam's example revealed that, while intelligence may be genetic, wisdom is not.

Rehoboam had the perfect opportunity and was set up for success. When he succeeded his father as the king of Israel, the people pledged their loyalty with the single request that he would make their lives easier. The construction of the temple and the palace were complete, so the lifting of burdens was more than feasible.

To his credit, Rehoboam did not answer hastily but set aside three days to seek counsel. Even more, Rehoboam sought wise counsel, and wise counsel was provided. "And they said to him, 'If you will be a servant to this people today and serve them, and speak good words to them when you answer them, then they will be your servants forever'" (1 Kings 12:7). But wise counsel is useless when unheeded.

Rather than listen to the voices of wisdom and experience, Rehoboam also sought counsel from his young friends, who proved to be nothing more than an echo chamber for his terrible ideas and sinister motives. "But he abandoned the counsel that the old men gave him and took counsel with the young men who had grown up with him and stood before him" (1 Kings 12:8). Their advice wasn't automatically foolish simply because they were young, but their immaturity and inexperience surely led to their sorry advice.

Rather than serve the people, Rehoboam made known his oppressive intentions. "He spoke to them according to the counsel of the young men, saying, 'My father made your yoke heavy, but I will add to your yoke. My father disciplined you with whips, but I will discipline you with scorpions'" (1 Kings 12:14). No one could accuse Rehoboam of diplomacy; but what Rehoboam lacked in diplomacy, he made up for with hardheaded arrogance.

Rehoboam's foolishness brought about the split of the kingdom as the unified nation of Israel became the divided nations of Israel and Judah. The Bible reassures us that this was all part of God's plan, but God's sovereignty neither takes Rehoboam off the hook nor removes the need for us to learn from his foolishness.

We need wise and Godly counsel - not just when we are facing major decisions but in our day-to-day living. That counsel is, of course, always available to us in the Scriptures but only if we read and obey them. But along with His Word, God continues to impart His wisdom to His people. He uses all of our experiences - but especially our suffering - to grow us in wisdom and in effectiveness in helping others.

If we will do our part to seek out Godly counsel, we will find it. Proverbs 13:20 reminds us, "Whoever walks with the wise becomes wise, but the companion of fools will suffer harm." We never reach the point at which we no longer need the wisdom and perspective we receive from doing life together with brothers and sisters in Christ. Sometimes we won't appreciate what they have to say. Sometimes we must hear that we're wrong or terribly misguided. Other times we receive a measure of assurance that we're indeed moving in the right direction. Wise counsel, based in the Scriptures, keeps us from wrecking ourselves and enlarges our perspective. You were never meant to do this alone.

"Blessed is the man who walks not in the counsel of the wicked,
nor stands in the way of sinners,
nor sits in the seat of scoffers; but his delight is in the law of the LORD,
and on his law he meditates day and night."
Psalm 1:1–2

HEAD TO HEART

- From whom do you seek Godly counsel and wisdom in big and small decisions?

- How can you look to grow in wisdom and avoid repeating the mistakes you see others make?

- How has God used your experiences and the lessons learned from them to help and encourage someone else?

GEHAZI: OBLIGATORY GRACE

READING: 2 KINGS 5

FOCUS: *2 Kings 5:20 "Gehazi, the servant of Elisha the man of God, said, 'See, my master has spared this Naaman the Syrian, in not accepting from his hand what he brought. As the LORD lives, I will run after him and get something from him.'"*

We know that some diseases are extremely contagious, but what if diseases could be exchanged? Not in the sense that a person could have one disease and trade up for a more enjoyable condition, but what if a person with a disease could gift the infirmity to someone else? At the beginning of 2 Kings 5, Naaman, the Syrian commander, had leprosy. By the end of the same chapter, Gehazi, the servant of Elisha, had leprosy. The plot twist is that Naaman no longer suffered from leprosy, but now Gehazi did. Naaman received the better end of that deal, but what happened?

The short answer is that Gehazi first suffered from a condition known as greed. But Elisha's servant did more than try to get what he wanted; Gehazi cheapened something much more valuable. Perhaps you remember Naaman's story. Desperate for healing from his leprous condition, Naaman was sent to the helpless king of Israel who referred him to the prophet Elisha. Despite being at first annoyed by Elisha's instructions to dip himself seven times in the Jordan River, Naaman decided that healing was worth a few moments of feeling ridiculous. When Naaman came up out of the water for the seventh time, the indignity was quickly forgotten and the leprosy was gone.

A humbled and grateful Naaman wanted to pay Elisha for the miracle, but Elisha adamantly refused the offer. "But he said, 'As the LORD lives, before whom I stand, I will receive none.' And he urged him to take it, but he refused" (2 Kings 5:16). Naaman's restoration was a gift of grace, and even he acknowledged the true Giver of his healing. But where Elisha saw an opportunity to show grace, his servant Gehazi simply saw an opportunity. "As the LORD lives, I will run after him and get something from him" (2 Kings 5:20b). Elisha gave, but Gehazi looked to get.

Before we even get to the getting, Gehazi was already playing with fire, invoking the Name of the Lord to support his own agenda. Gehazi may never have uttered the word "damn," but He was using God's Name in vain. He then broke another commandment with a lie. "And he said, 'All is well. My master has sent me to say, "There have just now come to me from the hill country of Ephraim two young men of the sons of the prophets. Please give them a talent of silver and two changes of clothing'" (2 Kings 5:22). No visitors had arrived, and no request had been made. With that, grace stopped being grace and was now an obligation. Naaman had no complaints about meeting the request, but that wasn't the issue. The miracle was no longer a gift.

When Elisha asked him where he had been, Gehazi said, "Your servant went nowhere." The lie Gehazi had told previously to Naaman was far more convincing. (Maybe the dog had eaten his homework also?) Gehazi should've realized that prophets know things that they aren't supposed to know. Whether the Lord had revealed Gehazi's scheme or Elisha knew by other means, Elisha wasn't fooled. "But he said to him, 'Did not my heart go when the man turned from his chariot to meet you? Was it a time to accept money and garments, olive orchards and vineyards, sheep and oxen, male servants and female servants?'" (2 Kings 5:26). This was not the time to receive a kickback but to dispense grace.

When we read about the consequences for Gehazi, our first inclination might be to see the consequences as harsh. We feel the heaviness of

Elisha's words: "Therefore the leprosy of Naaman shall cling to you and to your descendants forever" (2 Kings 5:27a). But who hasn't been a little greedy? Who doesn't want to be compensated fairly? If that was the crime, then we'd have one big leper colony. Greed was the motivation but not the heart of the problem. The deeper sin was that Gehazi turned what God gave as a gift into a debt to be repaid.

More than likely, Naaman had previously victimized the people of Israel. His servant girl had been abducted from her family in Israel. Especially given Naaman's initial reaction, Elisha could have told him to go dunk himself in one of the Syrian rivers and see if he received healing there. Instead God used his servant Elisha to grant healing to Naaman because that's how grace works, gushing like a river to the most undeserving. If undeserving was the criteria, Naaman was overqualified. Grace doesn't need to be repaid and cannot be repaid - even by our best efforts. Rather than imposing a new or a different obligation, grace sets us free.

Gehazi suffered for putting a price on grace, but do we do the same? If we are trying to somehow pay God back or if we're trying to leverage His favor with our good behavior, we aren't walking in His grace. Jesus is the Gospel, and no supplements are needed. Jesus paid it all. You've been set free. That's the good news. That's God's grace.

> *"And call upon me in the day of trouble;*
> *I will deliver you, and you shall glorify me."*
> Psalm 50:15

HEAD TO HEART

- Why do you think Gehazi's consequence was the same as Naaman's previous condition?

- Why was trying to change God's gift into a debt to be repaid such an awful action?

• In what ways have you been tempted, or have you tried to repay God? "Jesus plus" what?

JEHU: SELECTIVELY ZEALOUS

READING: 2 KINGS 10:18-36

FOCUS: *2 Kings 10:28-29 "Thus Jehu wiped out Baal from Israel. But Jehu did not turn aside from the sins of Jeroboam the son of Nebat, which he made Israel to sin— that is, the golden calves that were in Bethel and in Dan."*

Once the kingdoms of Israel and Judah had divided, King Jehu of Israel was arguably the best king that Israel ever had. Unfortunately, that was also the equivalent to being the best player on a winless team. Jehu was marginal, where all the others were awful. If nothing else, Jehu advanced the cause of mediocrity.

But weren't there some good kings in the Old Testament? Weren't there any Godly leaders? Yes, but they were all kings of Judah. Kings such as Hezekiah, Josiah and Jehoshaphat were, for the most part, strong and courageous leaders for Judah - not Israel. This is part of the reason why Israel did not last as long as Judah and was eventually conquered and enslaved by the Assyrians. (2 Kings 17)

Once the nation of Israel had split into the kingdoms of Israel and Judah, Jeroboam was the first king of Israel. You might recall that Rehoboam's lack of judgment and discretion led to the rebellion that brought about that division (1 Kings 12), so we would hope that Jeroboam would be better than Rehoboam. Sadly, he was not and set the bar exceedingly low for all the kings who would follow.

Jeroboam left no doubt about what kind of king he would be when he immediately set up golden calves at Dan in the north and Bethel in the south for the people of Israel to worship. 1 Kings 12:28 says, "So the king took counsel and made two calves of gold. And he said to the people, 'You have gone up to Jerusalem long enough. Behold your gods, O Israel, who brought you up out of the land of Egypt.'" Considering those golden calves were not fashioned until hundreds of years *after* the Exodus, we can safely conclude that either those were supremely talented bovines or Jeroboam had acted foolishly. (Jeroboam could have his own entry in this devotional!)

Fast forward many years and at least eight kings later to Jehu. Idolatry was not only still present in Israel but was evident in even more ways. Baal worship had become prevalent - helped along primarily by Ahab and Jezebel. (1 Kings 16:29-33) To his credit, Jehu held a special hatred for Baal worship. He set a trap for the priests of Baal and had them slaughtered. Jehu then tore down the temple of Baal and ensured that the temple ruins would be used as a latrine from that point on. And for good measure, Jehu ordered that Jezebel be thrown out of a window and trampled on by horses until her body was all but obliterated. Jehu was brutal but effective against the idolatry of Baal worship.

But evidently Jehu's zeal was more against Baal worship than *for* Yahweh. Jehu obviously had some tremendous zeal and an appropriate hatred for Baal and the false gods. Turning the temple of Baal into a latrine was an especially nice touch. He really flushed them out. But Jehu's passionate zeal against idolatry was also selective. He evidently did not burn with the same intensity against the golden calves, which were also idols. Instead of purging all of the idolatry from the land, Jehu turned a blind eye to the bovines.

2 Kings 10:30–31 reads, "And the LORD said to Jehu, 'Because you have done well in carrying out what is right in my eyes, and have done to the house of Ahab according to all that was in my heart, your sons of the fourth generation shall sit on the throne of Israel.' But Jehu was not careful to walk in the law of the LORD, the God of Israel, with all his heart. He did not turn from the sins of Jeroboam, which he made

Israel to sin." A zeal against some sin wasn't enough when other sin was being tolerated.

Pointing out Jehu's hypocrisy and inconsistency is all too easy. Recognizing those same tendencies in ourselves is a bigger challenge. We are all experts in selective obedience and being passionate only about the things that we happen to care about. We can have all the zeal to purge the world from what offends us and yet tolerate other things that God also sees as evil. Sin is so much easier to identify in someone else. May the Lord reveal to us the areas where our obedience is weak and half-hearted and where we are accommodating the things that God calls sin.

> *"Teach me your way, O LORD, that I may walk in your truth;*
> *unite my heart to fear your name. I give thanks to you,*
> *O Lord my God, with my whole heart,*
> *and I will glorify your name forever."*
> Psalm 86:11–12

HEAD TO HEART

- What makes one form of idolatry loathsome and another apparently acceptable?

- What sins and failures do you tend to recognize easily in others?

- What areas of sin and disobedience do you tend to tolerate in your life?

JEHORAM:
THE FALLOUT OF SIN

READING: 2 CHRONICLES 21

FOCUS: *2 Chronicles 21:20 "He was thirty-two years old when he began to reign, and he reigned eight years in Jerusalem. And he departed with no one's regret. They buried him in the city of David, but not in the tombs of the kings."*

When Jehoram succeeded his father Jehoshaphat as king, the groundwork had been laid by the faithfulness of his father. Jehoram could have easily just followed in the footsteps of the great Jehoshaphat and at least enjoyed a measure of success and effectiveness. Jehoram became the king by default since he was the oldest of several brothers. Even more, Jehoshaphat blessed his sons with riches. "Their father gave them great gifts of silver, gold, and valuable possessions, together with fortified cities in Judah, but he gave the kingdom to Jehoram, because he was the firstborn" (2 Chronicles 21:3).

Proverbs 22:6 says, "Train up a child in the way he should go; even when he is old he will not depart from it." We must understand, however, that this is a proverb - not an inviolable law. Exceptions happen. Generally speaking, Godly parents raise Godly children; but this is not always the case. Within the same family, sometimes two of the three children grow up to love Jesus; but the other child walks away from the faith. Other times, a child - without a great spiritual upbringing - becomes an amazing servant of the Lord. As parents, we do our best and trust the Lord; but since there are no guaranteed outcomes, we pray . . . a lot.

Surely Jehoshaphat did not attain perfection as a parent, but no one could have anticipated the man that his eldest son would become. "When Jehoram had ascended the throne of his father and was established, he killed all his brothers with the sword, and also some of the princes of Israel" (2 Chronicles 21:4). The level of insecurity and paranoia required to act in this way is hard for us to understand. The baffling aspect of this is that Jehoram was already and rightfully the king with no valid reason to be so paranoid. But Jehoram wasn't finished doing evil. "And he walked in the way of the kings of Israel, as the house of Ahab had done, for the daughter of Ahab was his wife. And he did what was evil in the sight of the LORD" (2 Chronicles 21:6). As the king of Judah, Jehoram was so bad that he was compared to the kings of Israel and specifically to Ahab, who was perhaps the worst of all.

Jehoram was a bad man; but he was on a leash, with God still ultimately in control. "Yet the LORD was not willing to destroy the house of David, because of the covenant that he had made with David, and since he had promised to give a lamp to him and to his sons forever" (2 Chronicles 21:7). David was long since dead and gone, but God would keep the promise He made to David. Thus, the wheels of God's justice began turning, and the end for Jehoram would be especially ugly.

The reckoning for Jehoram did not come suddenly or as a surprise. The prophet Elijah sent a letter to Jehoram, and it was not fan mail. Elijah penned the words of the Lord: "Because you have not walked in the ways of Jehoshaphat your father, or in the ways of Asa king of Judah, but have walked in the way of the kings of Israel and have enticed Judah and the inhabitants of Jerusalem into whoredom, as the house of Ahab led Israel into whoredom, and also you have killed your brothers, of your father's house, who were better than you, behold, the LORD will bring a great plague on your people, your children, your wives, and all your possessions" (2 Chronicles 21:12–14).

Jehoram got away with nothing. The evil he was committing did not go unnoticed by God, and a great plague was promised. But that wasn't all. The plague was general, but additional and specific consequences awaited Jehoram himself. What was the fallout for Jehoram's sin? His *bowels*. "And you yourself will have a severe sickness with a disease of your bowels, until your bowels come out because of the disease, day by day" (2 Chronicles 21:15). While a disease of the bowels sounds unpleasant, the falling out of the bowels "day by day" adds a special dimension of misery. The author wanted to make sure we knew that all of this happened as well. "And after all this the LORD struck him in his bowels with an incurable disease. In the course of time, at the end of two years, his bowels came out because of the disease, and he died in great agony. His people made no fire in his honor, like the fires made for his fathers. . . . And he departed with no one's regret . . ." (2 Chronicles 21:18–20a).

We could read the story of Jehoram as a cautionary tale, warning us against evil; but we can do better. First, the story was not a tale but actually happened. Secondly, we can be deeply comforted by what happened to Jehoram. Evil seems to go unchecked for a time, but God sees and knows. Evil will not ultimately prevail - let alone evil rulers. They make a lot of noise and cause destruction, but soon they are cast aside. They will all suffer the consequences for their actions - even if the fallout is not necessarily their bowels. When you get discouraged by the darkness you see in the world today, be assured that God wins and God rules.

> *". . . for those who honor me I will honor,*
> *and those who despise me shall be lightly esteemed."*
> 1 Samuel 2:30b

HEAD TO HEART

- How could Jehoshaphat be so good and Jehoram, his son, so evil?

- What can a parent do to guard against raising up a Jehoram?

- How do you stay hopeful and joyful in the midst of the darkness and evil in the world?

ATHALIAH: A REASON FOR TREASON

READING: 2 CHRONICLES 22:10-23:21

FOCUS: *2 Chronicles 22:10 "Now when Athaliah the mother of Ahaziah saw that her son was dead, she arose and destroyed all the royal family of the house of Judah."*

Long before the Grinch tried to steal Christmas, someone else nearly succeeded in eliminating Christmas before the Incarnation ever occurred. But God had a plan, and God had made a promise; so He would save what the enemy tried to steal. Besides the plan from the very beginning to send Jesus in "the fullness of time" (Galatians 4:4), God also had made a promise to King David. David wanted to build a house for the Lord; but God said that instead He would build a house for David and that the "house" wasn't a tabernacle or a temple but rather a line of descendants that would culminate in the birth of Jesus. "And your house and your kingdom shall be made sure forever before me. Your throne shall be established forever" (2 Samuel 7:16).

God obviously kept His promise long after David was dead and gone since Jesus was indeed born. But at one point, the line of David was only one descendant away from extinction. If Joash had not been rescued and hidden away, the lineage would have been destroyed. In ways that we do not understand, God permits evil to exist and persist in this world for now; and yet He fulfills every one of His promises.

Athaliah was the only queen to rule over Judah or Israel in the Old Testament; but before we celebrate a win for women, Athaliah rivaled even the most wicked kings. She was married to King Jehoram until they had a "falling out" brought about by Jehoram. (2 Chronicles 21) After

Jehoram's death, their son Ahaziah reigned as king briefly; but Ahaziah was only a puppet king, with Athaliah pulling the strings. The Bible says of Ahaziah: "He also walked in the ways of the house of Ahab, for his mother was his counselor in doing wickedly" (2 Chronicles 22:3). When Ahaziah was put to death, his mother Athaliah unanimously elected herself as the queen of Judah.

"Now when Athaliah the mother of Ahaziah saw that her son was dead, she arose and destroyed all the royal family of the house of Judah" (2 Chronicles 22:10). The lineage of David was eliminated . . . almost. Even as Athaliah was committing unimaginable evil against her family, God was working behind the scenes to protect His promise. We probably don't remember Jehoshabeath at Christmas or any other time, but God used her to preserve His plan to send His Son. "But Jehoshabeath, the daughter of the king, took Joash the son of Ahaziah and stole him away from among the king's sons who were about to be put to death, and she put him and his nurse in a bedroom. Thus Jehoshabeath, the daughter of King Jehoram and wife of Jehoiada the priest, because she was a sister of Ahaziah, hid him from Athaliah, so that she did not put him to death" (2 Chronicles 22:11).

Joash was spared and hidden away while Athaliah ruled over Judah. This was another time that, from all appearances, evil had won. From a human standpoint, the promise God had made to David depended on the survival of one small child named Joash, and that all seemed to be very much in question. But in reality, God's plan was being held firmly together by His sovereign control and faithfulness. Athaliah's evil scheme had no chance of succeeding because God already had ordained a different outcome.

When Joash was just seven years old, Jehoiada the priest led and organized the insurrection to establish Joash as the king. "Then they brought out the king's son and put the crown on him and gave him the testimony. And they proclaimed him king, and Jehoiada and his sons anointed him, and they said, 'Long live the king'" (2 Chronicles 23:11). When Athaliah heard all of the celebration and realized what was happening, she was less than pleased. "And Athaliah tore her clothes and cried, 'Treason! Treason!'" (2 Chronicles 23:13b) Not only were Athaliah's words ironic, but they also revealed that she had no inkling that any descendant of the house of David had survived. Her plans were even further hindered when she was taken out of the temple and put to death. Joash would rule over Judah for the next 40 years; but more importantly, he continued the line of David.

Athaliah probably never realized that she was fighting against what God had promised, but her evil plot was foiled. Eight hundred years later, Herod would viciously attempt to destroy Jesus as an infant; but God intervened again. (Matthew 2:13-18) Even as we're horrified at the attempts to thwart God's plan and purpose, we celebrate in the assurance that all of them will fail.

So many times, evil seems to have the upper hand. But, as dark as the story of Athaliah may be, we're again reminded that evil won't ultimately win. If God can work through one obscure woman with a long name to save the day, we can never assume that He isn't right now working in ways that we don't see or know about to accomplish all His purposes. God keeps His promises, and He has everything at His disposal to honor His Word. Even when it seems as though all is lost, His Kingdom will come, and His will *will* be done.

"Then the LORD said to me,
'You have seen well, for I am watching over my word to perform it.'"
Jeremiah 1:12

HEAD TO HEART

• On what specific promises of God are you standing today?

- What are some of the doubts and distractions that can cause you to get discouraged?

- Is there a Jehoshabeath in your life whom God has used powerfully but in quiet and hidden ways?

AMAZIAH: CONSISTENTLY INCONSISTENT

READING: 2 CHRONICLES 25

FOCUS: *2 Chronicles 25:8 "But go, act, be strong for the battle. Why should you suppose that God will cast you down before the enemy? For God has power to help or to cast down."*

Among the many struggles that we have in seeking to walk with the Lord is inconsistency. Our intensity fades, and our zeal comes and goes. We see God working in our lives in powerful ways in some seasons and yet find a way to shoot ourselves in the foot in others. Amaziah was one of the kings of Judah, and his life was summed up this way: "And he did what was right in the eyes of the LORD, yet not with a whole heart" (2 Chronicles 25:2). While failure will often expose what is really in our hearts, our successes can do so to an even greater degree.

Amaziah was preparing to go to war with the Edomites with 300,000 select troops, who were battle-ready. But just in case that wasn't enough, he hired 100,000 mighty men from Israel. That may sound kosher, but Israel was no ally to Judah in those days. The hiring of fighting forces wasn't anything unusual, but seeking assistance from Israel was unwise and unnecessary. A man of God came to Amaziah and warned him that the Lord was not with Israel. These hired hands would likely hinder more than help. The words from the man of God to Amaziah were powerful. "But go, act, be strong for the battle. Why should you suppose that God will cast you down before the enemy? For God has power to help or to cast down" (2 Chronicles 25:8). Amaziah, go and fight. Why do you think that God won't help you here?

Before we go any further, let's pause to consider those words. Facing your own battles, do you have the confidence that God will accomplish His purpose and plan? Why should *you* suppose that God will cast you down before the enemy? Maybe you haven't gone out and hired an army, but have you formulated a contingency plan in case trusting God doesn't work out like you'd hoped? Even if things don't go the way you'd hoped and you are "cast down," may we be strong and trust God for whatever battle we're facing.

"But," Amaziah objected, "what about the money we've already paid to the soldiers of Israel?" Yes, that money would be wasted, and some would be angry that they were being sent home; but the man of God encouraged Amaziah to let it go. "The man of God answered, 'The LORD is able to give you much more than this'" (2 Chronicles 25:9b). With that, Amaziah wisely sent the troops of Israel home and engaged in the battle without them. He took courage and trusted in the Lord instead of his contingency plan, and Judah was victorious over the Edomites.

This was almost a great story about trusting the Lord and not our own wisdom. Amaziah was almost a great example of faith over fear - until he did the inexplicable. "After Amaziah came from striking down the Edomites, he brought the gods of the men of Seir and set them up as his gods and worshiped them, making offerings to them" (2 Chronicles 25:14). Having just defeated the Edomites in battle, Amaziah worshipped *their* gods. As the prophet said to Amaziah, "Why have you sought the gods of a people who did not deliver their own people from your hand?" (2 Chronicles 25:15b) But when did idolatry ever make sense?

How could Amaziah trust the Lord for one battle and then turn to idolatry? One clue to answering this question is the arrogance Amaziah displayed after he had conquered the Edomites. He was happy to receive God's help going into battle but then afterwards saw himself as the reason for the victory. Ironically, Amaziah later picked a fight with Israel but lost badly. The Bible tells us exactly why. ". . . for it was of God, in order that he might give them into the hand of their enemies, because they had sought the gods of Edom" (2 Chronicles 25:20b).

We have different battles to fight today, but what can we learn from Amaziah? On the front end of the battle, trust the Lord. No Plan B or contingency plans – trust Him. Go, act and be strong for the battle. When you're in the battle, keep trusting Him. And when the battle is won, give glory to the Lord. Also, our trust in the Lord yesterday isn't a given for today or tomorrow. New trials and temptations must be met with a renewed trust in the Lord. May you see His power displayed as you continually and consistently trust in His goodness.

"I will rejoice and be glad in your steadfast love,
because you have seen my affliction;
you have known the distress of my soul,
and you have not delivered me into the hand of the enemy;
you have set my feet in a broad place."
Psalm 31:7–8

HEAD TO HEART

- In what ways have you seen inconsistency in your walk with the Lord?

- Why would God allow Amaziah to have victory, knowing he would then turn to idols?

- Have you enjoyed victories or successes that have gone to your head?

UZZIAH: ONCE YOU'VE ARRIVED

READING: 2 CHRONICLES 26

FOCUS: *2 Chronicles 26:16 "But when he was strong, he grew proud, to his destruction. For he was unfaithful to the LORD his God and entered the temple of the LORD to burn incense on the altar of incense."*

"Vanity of vanities, says the Preacher, vanity of vanities! All is vanity" (Ecclesiastes 1:2). After those positive, encouraging words, the author of Ecclesiastes adds, "I have seen everything that is done under the sun, and behold, all is vanity and a striving after wind" (Ecclesiastes 1:14). Everything you do today could be just chasing the wind. And that idea isn't just an Old Testament concept. Paul speaks of all that God created being "subjected to futility" (Romans 8:20). We don't live a single day on this earth that we don't see multiple examples of futility. Doesn't that make you just want to break out in song?

People spend their lives chasing after money, possessions, experiences and success - only to discover that they are still lonely and empty even after they got what they thought they wanted. With those inspirational thoughts in mind, we turn to the story of Uzziah. Also called Azariah, Uzziah reigned over Judah for 52 years. (For American readers, imagine if President Nixon was still the president – that's 52 years ago!) For the majority of the time, Uzziah was solid. The narrator summarizes, "And he did what was right in the eyes of the LORD, according to all that his father Amaziah had done. He set himself to seek God in the days of Zechariah, who instructed him in the fear of God, and as long as he sought the LORD, God made him prosper" (2 Chronicles 26:4–5).

Times were comparatively good in Judah under Uzziah's reign. Judah was victorious in battle, and her enemies were paying tribute. Building projects were ongoing, while Uzziah amassed a large and well-equipped army. Uzziah must have been a capable and an effective leader, and kings of that caliber had been few and far between. "And his fame spread far, for he was marvelously helped, till he was strong" (2 Chronicles 26:15b). All seems to be well until the narrator added that last part – "till he was strong." Uh-oh.

We're tempted even now to believe that becoming strong and powerful is the goal. Once we're there, then we've really arrived. In the early days, Uzziah was dependent on the Lord. He feared God and sought Him. God was blessing and helping Uzziah so that Uzziah became strong as well as famous. Most of us will never know the degree of temptations that accompany the success that Uzziah had enjoyed. When we see ourselves as small and insignificant, we continually turn to the Lord for help. On the way up, we assume that nothing could ever change that . . . until we arrive.

While Uzziah could say that he reaped the blessings of many years of faithfulness, he did not finish well. Years of sizzle had deteriorated to fizzle, and Uzziah was never the same. Specifically, Uzziah became both arrogant and angry. "But when he was strong, he grew proud, to his destruction. For he was unfaithful to the LORD his God and entered the temple of the LORD to burn incense on the altar of incense" (2 Chronicles 26:16). Now burning incense in the temple doesn't sound like a heinous crime, but that specific task was reserved for the priests. Perhaps out of desperation - as Uzziah began to see things fall apart, he took it upon himself to make the offering. As the priests told him, "It is not for you, Uzziah, to burn incense to the LORD, but for the priests, the sons of Aaron, who are consecrated to burn incense. Go out of the sanctuary, for you have done wrong, and it will bring you no honor from the LORD God" (2 Chronicles 26:18b).

In the moment, Uzziah could have taken a breath, admitted he was wrong and walked away. Instead he got angry, and there is no rage like that of an entitled person being told no. Suddenly, Uzziah broke out with leprosy. The face that had been red with fury was now white with leprosy. If we have any suspicions about coincidences, the Bible immediately removes them. "And they rushed him out quickly, and he himself hurried to go out, because the LORD had struck him" (2 Chronicles 26:20b). As a leper to the day of his death, Uzziah would never enter the temple again.

You are probably safe from contracting leprosy today, but you might avoid armadillos just to be safe. None of us, however, have immunity to the more sinister disease of our foolish pride. Sometimes our circumstances help us stay humble, but sometimes our successes contribute to our pride. If God blesses you, stay humble and be deeply grateful. If He doesn't bless you in the way that you believe He should, He could be protecting you in ways you'll never know – perhaps even protecting you from yourself.

"You have given me the shield of your salvation, and your right hand supported me, and your gentleness made me great. You gave a wide place for my steps under me, and my feet did not slip."
Psalm 18:35–36

HEAD TO HEART

- Do you take credit for your successes but blame God or others for your failures?

- In what other ways have you seen people not being able to handle success?

- How do you protect your heart from pride when God has helped you to be successful?

MANASSEH: WHILE YOU STILL HAVE TIME

READING: 2 CHRONICLES 33:1-20

FOCUS: *2 Chronicles 33:13 "He prayed to him, and God was moved by his entreaty and heard his plea and brought him again to Jerusalem into his kingdom. Then Manasseh knew that the LORD was God."*

King Hezekiah had been a Godly king for Judah and one of the best. Despite some foolish decisions later in life, the Bible says of Hezekiah, "And he did what was right in the eyes of the LORD, according to all that David his father had done" (2 Chronicles 29:2). Hezekiah trusted the Lord in difficult days and against formidable enemies, and God blessed his obedience.

The Bible doesn't comment on Hezekiah's parenting; but sadly, all the good that Hezekiah accomplished was undone after Manasseh, his son, took over. Israel and Judah endured plenty of regrettable kings, but Manasseh was possibly the worst of them all. Unlike many of the other "train wrecks" who were quickly deposed, Manasseh reigned in Judah for 55 years. He had a long time to be terrible. Sometimes evil persists far longer than we thought God would have allowed, but Manasseh was never off the leash of God's rule and authority. The same applies to evil rulers today.

Manasseh's rap sheet was long and eventful. "And he did what was evil in the sight of the LORD, according to the abominations of the nations whom the LORD drove out before the people of Israel. For he rebuilt the high places that his father Hezekiah had broken down, and he erected altars to the Baals, and made Asheroth, and worshiped all the host of heaven and served them" (2 Chronicles 33:2–3). But he wasn't finished there. "And he burned his sons as an offering in the Valley of the Son of Hinnom, and used fortune-telling and omens and sorcery, and dealt with mediums and with necromancers. He did much evil in the sight of the LORD, provoking him to anger" (2 Chronicles 33:6).

Some people seem to think that sin was a recent invention; but when it comes to the depths of human depravity, there truly is "nothing new under the sun" (Ecclesiastes 1:9). Idolatry, astrology, child sacrifice, sorcery and occult activity were all a part of Manasseh's reign. But why didn't God intervene? Whatever happened to the wicked not prospering? The narrator summarizes: "Manasseh led Judah and the inhabitants of Jerusalem astray, to do more evil than the nations whom the LORD destroyed before the people of Israel" (2 Chronicles 33:9).

But finally, the leash ran out; and Manasseh was about to receive his due. "The LORD spoke to Manasseh and to his people, but they paid no attention. Therefore the LORD brought upon them the commanders of the army of the king of Assyria, who captured Manasseh with hooks and bound him with chains of bronze and brought him to Babylon" (2 Chronicles 33:10–11). The party was over. God could have struck Manasseh down at any point, but the consequences for Manasseh came at the hands of men. The Assyrians were known for being especially cruel to their enemies and were likely more so to a conquered king. With a hook perhaps through his nose or lips, Manasseh was led away to Babylon. Along with the pain Manasseh experienced, the king who had been brazenly wicked for so long was now humiliated.

The Bible contains plenty of ironies and surprises but possibly none more surprising than the next chapter of Manasseh's story. Even as we're satisfied that he was finally reaping the whirlwind for his evil practices, Manasseh did what no one would have ever expected. "And when he was in distress, he entreated the favor of the LORD his God and humbled himself greatly before the God of his fathers" (2 Chronicles 33:12). Manasseh humbled himself and cried out to God. Where had that been for the last 55 years? But even as we read about Manasseh's prayer, we may remain suspicious. Couldn't anyone fake contrition when they have a hook driven through their nose? Were they real or crocodile tears? So many have expressed grief over their consequences but not over the sin that brought them about.

But the Scriptures surprise us again. "He prayed to him, and God was moved by his entreaty and heard his plea and brought him again to Jerusalem into his kingdom. Then Manasseh knew that the LORD was God" (2 Chronicles 33:13). God again showed grace to one of the most undeserving. If we notice anything from Manasseh's story, *authentic humility moves the heart of God.* As astounding as it was, Manasseh humbled himself before God, and God heard his prayer. Not all of the consequences were removed, and Manasseh still went down as one of the worst rulers ever. But while he still could, Manasseh learned that the Lord is God.

God still grants repentance to some of the most unlikely. Criminals - like the one next to Jesus on the cross - still find forgiveness. Keep praying for those off in the far country. If Manasseh could still receive the grace to humble himself and repent, so can they . . . and so can we.

"For the LORD takes pleasure in his people;
he adorns the humble with salvation."
Psalm 149:4

HEAD TO HEART

- Do you think Manasseh's evil resulted from poor parenting or his own bad choices?

- Why doesn't God put an end to evil deeds and evil people sooner than He does?

- How would we know if someone's repentance is authentic rather than just hoping to avoid the consequences?

JOB & FRIENDS: WORDS WITHOUT WISDOM

READING: JOB 42

FOCUS: *Job 42:7 "After the LORD had spoken these words to Job, the LORD said to Eliphaz the Temanite: 'My anger burns against you and against your two friends, for you have not spoken of me what is right, as my servant Job has.'"*

Whenever we know the backstory or the history of how a situation developed, we have a much easier time in knowing what to say or do. The problem is that most of the time we don't. As the saying goes, "We don't know what we don't know." When we read the story of Job, we have the benefit of knowing what happened to Job in the first two chapters and, more importantly, why. To appreciate the rest of the story, we must keep in mind that Job and his friends knew nothing about the conversations that took place in the spiritual realm.

We discover right away what God Himself had to say about Job. "And the LORD said to Satan, 'Have you considered my servant Job, that there is none like him on the earth, a blameless and upright man, who fears God and turns away from evil?'" (Job 1:8) Would God say that about any of us? We also see that Satan challenged Job's faithfulness to God. "But stretch out your hand and touch all that he has, and he will curse you to your face" (Job 1:11). As Job's entire world fell apart in the verses that followed, we know that God was allowing Satan to test Job and that Satan could only do what God allowed him to do. But Job didn't know and couldn't know any of that. The only people even more in the dark than Job were his friends.

Eliphaz, Bildad and Zophar came to comfort Job in his affliction. For seven days, they sat with Job without saying a word because of the severity of Job's afflictions. Who wouldn't want friends in a time of crisis who understand that their presence is needed more than their words? To their credit, Job's friends wanted to help. When Job finally broke the silence, he began by cursing the day he was born and later wished that he had died right after birth. (Job 3) Job's dark and dreary soliloquy must have stirred up his friends as they too began to speak. For the next 34 chapters, Job engaged in long, poetic arguments with his opinionated friends about why all these calamities had happened. Each of them was partly right and yet mostly wrong.

Now, if we didn't know why Job was suffering, we might have sided with Job's friends. People do indeed reap what they sow. The essence of their arguments was that Job had sinned and that his suffering was God's retribution. Simple cause and effect. They reduced complexities to simple formulas based on limited understanding. To them, Job was suffering; so Job must have sinned. Like a long-winded preacher who can't "land the plane," they railed on and on about Job's sin and God's justice. Like someone you may know today, they were often wrong but never in doubt.

For example, Eliphaz scolded, "Behold, blessed is the one whom God reproves; therefore despise not the discipline of the Almighty" (Job 5:17). Then Bildad offered his counsel: "If you will seek God and plead with the Almighty for mercy, if you are pure and upright, surely then he will rouse himself for you and restore your rightful habitation" (Job 8:5–6). Zophar added this little nugget of encouragement: "Know then that God exacts of you less than your guilt deserves" (Job 11:6b). None of Job's friends probably were ever invited to write the messages used in sympathy cards.

But even as we empathize with his anguish, Job was in the wrong as well. At first, Job "did not sin or charge God with wrong" (Job 1:22b).

Where his friends assumed the tragedies happened because God was not pleased, Job later argued they happened because God was not just. Job's contentions in Job 9 are painful to read. If you've ever listened to someone spew the fury of their pain, disappointment and confusion, you can recognize the anguish in Job's words. "If I summoned him and he answered me, I would not believe that he was listening to my voice. For he crushes me with a tempest and multiplies my wounds without cause; he will not let me get my breath, but fills me with bitterness" (Job 9:16–18).

Throughout the lengthy chapters of Job, we're not expected to agree with what Job is contending but to simply hear his pain. Again, Job didn't know why this was happening. He knew he had no secret sin or overt transgression, so how could God be doing this to him? In perhaps his lowest moment of all, Job contends, "It is all one; therefore I say, 'He destroys both the blameless and the wicked.' When disaster brings sudden death, he mocks at the calamity of the innocent. The earth is given into the hand of the wicked; he covers the faces of its judges—if it is not he, who then is it?" (Job 9:22–24) For Job, if God wasn't to blame, who was?

Although Job believed and said some wrong things, he never walked away from God. He held on, waiting for a divine explanation. But Job never got an explanation – what Job got instead was God. After 35 chapters of painful monologues, God powerfully ended His silence, but He didn't explain or apologize. In mysterious but not uncertain terms, God flattened Job with the reality that God was God, and Job was not. Before a single thing was restored to Job, Job humbly praised the Creator and acknowledged that he had "uttered what I did not understand, things too wonderful for me, which I did not know" (Job 42:3b). Once Job had seen God, he concluded, "therefore I despise myself, and repent in dust and ashes" (Job 42:6).

God had humbled Job and yet vindicated him at the same time. In contrast, Job's friends were not vindicated but silenced. As God told them, "And my servant Job shall pray for you, for I will accept his prayer not to deal with you according to your folly. For you have not spoken of me what is right, as my servant Job has" (Job 42:8b). God restored to Job all of his blessings; but even if He had not, Job was content with the greatness of God and with knowing that some things were beyond his understanding.

While we will inevitably endure suffering in this life, may we not have to undergo what Job did to grasp what Job learned. God is God, and we are not. God does things and allows things that we don't understand; but He is good. Our perspective on our lives is very limited, so how much more limited is our perspective on the lives of other people? Before we rant and rave in ignorance about someone's suffering or even our own, we must have the humility to remember that we surely don't have the complete picture. Job suffered, but he was never abandoned.

Many years later, Jesus would suffer — even more than Job. Jesus wouldn't feel forsaken; He would be forsaken. But Jesus chose the suffering. He chose the cross. He entered the same broken world of suffering in which Job once lived and in which you live now. We don't get to know all of the answers; but we know that Jesus suffered for us, and now Jesus suffers with us. When our understanding is not sufficient, His grace is.

"Then the LORD answered Job out of the whirlwind and said:
'Dress for action like a man; I will question you,
and you make it known to me. Will you even put me in the wrong?
Will you condemn me that you may be in the right? Have you an arm
like God, and can you thunder with a voice like his?'"
Job 40:6–9

HEAD TO HEART

- In what ways does your story resemble and differ from Job's?

- What do Job's friends teach us about ministering to those who are hurting?

- In what areas of your life do you need the continual reminder that you aren't God?

THE SERPENT:
THE ULTIMATE FAILURE

READING: GENESIS 3

FOCUS: *Genesis 3:14–15 "The LORD God said to the serpent, 'Because you have done this, cursed are you above all livestock and above all beasts of the field; on your belly you shall go, and dust you shall eat all the days of your life. I will put enmity between you and the woman, and between your offspring and her offspring; he shall bruise your head, and you shall bruise his heel.'"*

The Old Testament is many different stories that make up a single narrative, but that story is not one of success or victory. By only the third chapter of the Bible, the failure had begun already, and the effects of the resulting curse are seen in various ways from Genesis through Malachi. A few Godly men and women lived lives that glorified God, but Israel had failed to be what God had intended. Most of the time, they had not loved God, had not kept His commandments and had not been an example and a blessing to the other nations. If anything, Israel had been an ongoing example of what happens when the people of God turn to the false gods and idols of the nations.

What began so gloriously in Genesis was corrupted so quickly. God created the world and saw that it was good. God created the man and the woman and saw that they were good. But with only one possible way that they could fail, Adam and Eve succeeded in failure. Only one thing had been prohibited, but they just had to have the fruit of that tree. They too had one job.

But in all fairness, Adam and Eve had help. They didn't wake up that morning with the intention of ruining the entire world. "Now the serpent was more crafty than any other beast of the field that the LORD God had made" (Genesis 3:1a). Satan used the same tactics with the woman that he still uses today. He caused them to doubt what God had said. He made the forbidden fruit look even more appealing. He made big promises about the benefits. "So when the woman saw that the tree was good for food, and that it was a delight to the eyes, and that the tree was to be desired to make one wise, she took of its fruit and ate, and she also gave some to her husband who was with her, and he ate" (Genesis 3:6).

The story of the Fall is familiar enough to most of us that we can miss some things because we already know how the story turns out. Why watch a train wreck over and over again? But have you ever wondered what the serpent was thinking when God didn't kill Adam and Eve, when they didn't immediately die (at least physically) after they ate the fruit? We can't know precisely what Satan did and didn't know, but sometimes he's given too much credit. He's crafty, but he's not omniscient. The serpent knew that he had succeeded in getting them to break the one rule, but what did he think when God came to find them when they were trying to hide? What went through the serpent's evil mind when later God Himself clothed Adam and Eve to cover their newly discovered shame? When Adam named his wife Eve, which means "life giver," after they had sinned, was Satan scratching his scaly head?

When God "found" Adam and Eve, the time had come for the consequences to be announced. But if Satan didn't already know what was coming, this may have been the biggest surprise of all. Maybe Satan really believed that he had foiled all of God's plans, that he had won. But God didn't start with the consequences for Adam or Eve. They did the crime, but the curse came first for the serpent. "The LORD God said to the serpent, 'Because you have done this, cursed are you above all livestock and above all beasts of the field; on your belly you shall go, and dust you shall eat all the days of your life. I will put enmity between you and the woman, and between your offspring and her offspring; he shall bruise your head, and you shall bruise his heel'" (Genesis 3:14–15).

Although everything had fallen apart, in the very curse God pronounced on the serpent, we see the first announcement of the Gospel. No, God didn't spell out the entire plan and all of the details; but it was nonetheless a preview of redemption. Could there still be reason for hope? God said that He would put enmity between the serpent and the woman as well as enmity between their offspring. But notice the word for offspring (or literally, seed) is singular, not plural as in "seeds" or "offsprings." The Lord went on to say, "He shall bruise your head, and you shall bruise His heel." Thus, the Seed of the woman would bruise (or "crush" in some translations) the head of the serpent.

Just as a snake will do even now, the serpent would strike the heel of the woman's Seed; but He would stomp the serpent's head into the ground. Maybe Satan knew what it all meant, or maybe he didn't; but God was making clear that the final victory wouldn't be his. From the beginning, God already had made provision for all that Adam and Eve's epic failure made necessary. Even as Paradise had just been lost, God already was proclaiming that victory over sin and death would come through Jesus, the Seed of the woman. Jesus, by His death and resurrection, crushed the head of the enemy.

Yes, the world in many ways was ruined by the Fall; and yes, there were still consequences for Adam and Eve. When we read about the curses, we tend to think with sadness of all the things that would never be the same again. But that's not true. When Jesus came, the reverse of the curse began. God is restoring what He intended all along. We see things continuing to deteriorate as the Day approaches; and we see the many ways that the serpent - still squirming and slithering like a snake with his head chopped off - is even now a defeated enemy. Just as one man's disobedience set in motion the brokenness of the world, Jesus made the way for the curse to be reversed and for all things to be made new.

We've seen plenty of failures in the Old Testament. Even some of our Bible heroes revealed their feet of clay, but the most colossal and ultimate failure was that of the serpent. He wreaked havoc and so often seemed to have the upper hand, but his fate was already sealed. Our redemption plan was set in motion, and God's purposes will stand.

All too often, our feet of clay remind us that we too are broken by sin. On some days, our failure rivals the foolish choices of the people in the Old Testament. But remember, the serpent's evil scheme already has failed. The battle is over, and Jesus won. Sin and death remain for now, but they will not have the final word. Look to the Old Testament to learn from their failures; but as you do, look to Jesus the Author and Finisher of our faith.

"For to us a child is born, to us a son is given;
and the government shall be upon his shoulder,
and his name shall be called Wonderful Counselor,
Mighty God, Everlasting Father, Prince of Peace.
Of the increase of his government and of peace there will be no end,
on the throne of David and over his kingdom,
to establish it and to uphold it with justice
and with righteousness from this time forth and forevermore.
The zeal of the LORD of hosts will do this."
Isaiah 9:6–7

HEAD TO HEART

• When you see the results of the enemy's work, are you still able to see him as defeated?

- Even in Adam and Eve's consequences, in what ways do we see God's mercy?

- Of all the characters we've studied, with whom did you identify and learn from the most?

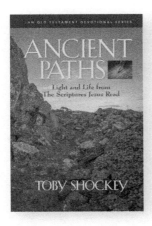 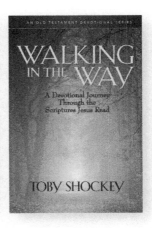

Made in the USA
Middletown, DE
27 September 2022

11262898R00080